MW01488447

Bamboo Bending

Bamboo Bending

*An Educator's Changing
Corner of the Universe*

Morgan Zo Callahan

Morgan Zo Callahan was born in New York City, studied at Jesuit schools, received an MA in Philosophy at Gonzaga University, took courses in political philosophy at Stanford University's Hoover Institute, and trained as a community organizer at the Alinsky Institute in Chicago. For eighteen years he taught mental fitness at convalescent hospitals, where he became interested in hospice work. Currently he teaches high-school SAT English and adult-school ESL. He's been fortunate to have traveled widely, meeting along the way many wonderful, interesting people in Taiwan, Korea, Mexico, El Salvador, Spain, Morocco, Costa Rica, Canada, Guatemala, Panama, Nicaragua, Honduras, Italy, the Bahamas, Haiti, and the Dominican Republic. Morgan is the author of *Red Buddhist Envelope* and the co-author of *Intimate Meanderings: Conversations Close to Our Hearts*, published by iUniverse.

Copyright © 2014 Morgan Zo Callahan

All rights reserved. No part of this publication may be reproduced, stored in or introduced into a retrieval system, or transmitted in any form or by any means (electronic, mechanical, by photocopying, recording or otherwise) without the prior written permission of the author.

ISBN-10: 1-4942-3717-2
ISBN-13: 978-1-4942-3717-2

Questions or comments can be directed to
BambooBending@gmail.com

The original cover image, the painting "Bamboo Bending," is used courtesy of the artist.
Copyright © 2014 Lu Che

This book is dedicated to my mother and father, Daniel Berrigan, Greg Boyle, Malala Yousafzai, and Matthew Shepard.

My brother used to bless the birds,
and it is right that he should do so.
All is like an ocean blending;
a touch set up in one corner of the
universe affects everything else.
(Fr. Zossima to Alyosha in
The Brothers Karamazov)
—Fyodor Dostoyevsky

Table of Contents

Foreword

At the heart of each thoughtful person is a wellspring of energy, creative hope, and purposeful drive that opens and bubbles forth when the teaching-learning dialogue touches the lives, souls, and minds of two or more people. Morgan Zo Callahan dives into this encounter with his students, surviving and learning from dangerous risks and uncertain situations. He begins his educator's journey with a street mugging that might have come out of Gregory Boyle's gang tales in *Tattoos on the Heart*. We experience daring and courage first hand with Morgan as guide, as we enter the lives of students who live by the law of the streets. We hear high school/adult school educational theory, Buddhist mindfulness, and meet young Hispanics, new Asian immigrants, Chinese students and parents, the elderly, hospice patients, and those in therapy. Amy Chua's Tiger Moms appear in passionate stories of loving yet sometimes enraged Chinese-American students. Originally Hispanics were the largest minority in the San Gabriel Valley school districts, but over the past decade the largest minority is now Asian students.

This East-Coast raised, California-Jesuit-educated writer uses Saul Alinsky's methods to organize efforts to confront and transcend the obstacles that litter US education. Together we can carve new pathways for teenagers who ride emotional roller coasters as they try to navigate our confusing American culture. The bamboo of our minds and emotions must bend to move the student-learner, whole and alive, toward maturity. Mixed with readings in educational literature and anecdotes from lives of students, this mosaic of stories narrates his own ups and downs in educational and cultural playing fields, which map a journey into adult life. "I am so fortunate," Morgan writes, "a co-teacher with my students, co-learners on this wild, unpredictable journey through life."

Meditation practice finds the body's center for enlightenment and self-emptying of useless detours. "Meditation," we are reminded, comes from Latin and Greek words "to cure," "to care for." Brain studies and insights from developmental psychology guide us through teen minds and emotions, social and personal expressions, and verbal and non-verbal communication. We visit Mexico through Matraca, a service for street children in Xalapa, Veracruz; and we witness the struggles of the impoverished people in Chiapas as well as of indigenous people converging on Mexico City to march for human rights.

US education has been examined and reexamined for its successes and failures, challenged by its present mediocre rank in world statistics. I have been part of it for forty-five years at high school and college levels, and remain a trustee for five elementary schools for the Archdiocese of New York. I also coached young men and women in five sports during my teaching years. I see links between teaching and coaching, mostly for motivation and transfer of energies and interests. *Bamboo Bending* wrestles with our US educational challenges and invites the reader to enter into its wonders and join the search that aims for a mature humanity.

John B. Lounibos, PhD
Blauvelt, New York

Preface

Students, optimistic yet wary about their future, asked me to write about my life as a teacher and volunteer. Many observers say our education system is nearly broken by the stormy winds of our times; but my teaching experience, now primarily with Chinese-American students, tells me that if we work wisely we can be as resilient as the Chinese principal commodity, bamboo. We will not break, but gently bend as we evolve as agents for productive change. Beautiful Chinese calligraphies sometimes accompany paintings of bamboo—a symbol of longevity, strength, durability, and flexibility because of its wide-ranging uses: food, utensils, paper, furniture, building material, matting, clothing, transportation, weapons, decorations and plaintive musical instruments. "China is not only famous for its natural treasure, the giant panda, but also the giant panda's staple food—bamboo. The Chinese love bamboo, and bamboo culture has been rooted in their minds for a long time. To the Chinese people, bamboo is a symbol of virtue. It reflects people's souls and emotions, harmony between nature and human beings."[1]

Bamboo Bending pays tribute to the flexible, soulful strength that I find in my high school and adult students, an experience that makes me positive about the future. This book takes you through my life as a teacher and volunteer, with its successes and mistakes. It is also a conversation about technological and neuroscientific advances applied to education and a proposal for lifelong learning in our rapidly changing interconnected world. In this collaborative plan for the future of education—involving my students, their parents, their teachers, and me—you will read how life's events and experiences formed my philosophy.

---

[1] http://www.chinaculture.org/2011-01/04/content_443114.htm

Together all of us concerned with educating our children can design an effective blueprint for a state-of-the-art, holistic, globally accessible high-school education.

Respecting their privacy, I have changed most names and identifying details of the people in this memoir.

Acknowledgments

> *I live my life in widening circles*
> *that reach out across the world.*
> *I may not complete the last one*
> *but I give myself to it.*
> —Rainer Maria Rilke

Thank you, esteemed reader. I am deeply grateful to my high school and adult students, family, friends, and Dori, my wife from Taiwan, who has taught me about the rich Chinese culture and the importance of EQ. Recently I edited attorney Sanford Perliss's *A Thousand Invisible Cords: An American Lawyer's Unorthodox Journey*, unusual stories of practicing immigration and criminal law for the Chinese community in the San Gabriel Valley. Reversing roles, Sanford, whose wife is also from Taiwan, found windows in his busy schedule, to patiently and astutely edit *Bamboo Bending*. I appreciate his expertise, wise counsel, and friendship.

With gratitude to the *Compañeros-as*; Ken Ireland, editor and co-author of *Intimate Meanderings*; John Lounibos, Michael Saso, Ken Rose, Don Foran, James Won for expert proofreading, Gary Schouborg for valuable editing, Lu Che for her beautiful cover painting, Jeremy Rahl for the cover design, and Robert R. Rahl, adept copy editor and book designer; and to colleagues, teachers and students of: Gonzaga University; Hoover Institute, Stanford University; Bellarmine College Prep, San Jose; Saul Alinsky Institute, Chicago; PICO; New College of California; California Institute of Integral Studies, San Francisco; The Laughing Man Institute, San Francisco; Fairfield School of San Francisco; St. Lucy's High School, Glendora; El Centro Community Health Center; Loyola Institute of Spirituality; Top League Institute; El Monte-Rosemead Adult School; and Baldwin Park Adult School.

Introduction

A human being is a part of the whole called by us "the universe," a part limited in time and space. He experiences himself, his thoughts and feelings as something separate from the rest—a kind of optical delusion of his consciousness. This delusion is a kind of prison for us, restricting us to our personal desires and affection for a few persons nearest us. Our task must be to free ourselves from this prison by widening our circle of understanding and compassion to embrace all living creatures and the whole of nature in its beauty.
—Albert Einstein

On a blue-black night, I looked up at a bright silvery moon. Taking a deep breath, I felt I could touch distant stars and launch myself through limitless skies in a universe stretching fourteen billion years, all being, an infinity of causes and effects, continually evolving, inter-acting, exploding, giving birth, subsisting, dying and transforming. Closely related in a luminescent, mysterious process, beyond our capacity to fully know, our existence brings us joys as well as disasters we cannot fathom or control. Extreme, shocking and distressing events can awaken us from our daily routine and arouse a new and dramatic perspective. We are interdependent and connected to everything and everyone, even to that which is abhorrent—the most violent and hostile of our species. That which is in all people is likewise to some extent in me. I am a tiny participant, along with you, in this cosmic dancing with the stars.

Soon after I exited a 7-Eleven in Hollywood, just before dark, six enraged assailants ferociously attacked me. The police would later say I resembled an older version of a rival gang member, *hombre alto*, "tall man."

They did not go for my wallet. Full of vengeance, their objective was to kill me. I fought back as best I could. For a couple of years in the early 1980s, I learned basic taekwondo at Master Chun Lee's studio on Rosemead Boulevard, across from the Southeast Asian Refugee program, run by El Monte-Rosemead Adult School. Master Lee taught us self-defense: kicks, punches, footwork, a series of moves, attacking, and warding off blows. Despite that training, the end—though delayed a few moments—came quickly. I was punched, head-butted, and finally one of them plunged a long pearl-gray blade deep into my stomach, severing my renal vein and slicing my left kidney in half. Blood gushed from the wound. I credit Master Lee for his instruction. I was able to summon reflexive techniques to mitigate the effects of the vicious stabbing. When I stop by to say hi to Chun Lee, I feel gratitude and also chagrin that I didn't continue practicing taekwondo.

The thugs disappeared into a surreal twilight zone between life and death. I experienced the thin line separating passing out and somehow willfully hanging onto consciousness. For a few seconds of expansive awareness, a part of me rose into the sky and calmly floated above my body, a crumbling, bleeding mess. I pressed the wound in my stomach to stop the massive blood flow. Doctors later told me that, by putting pressure on my wound, I was the first in a team to save my life. To live, I needed to be saved by a Good Samaritan. Frightened passersby rushed from the desperate scene. Cars slowed and then screeched away, ignoring my pleas for help. A few drivers stopped, opened their doors, changed their minds and fled. For perhaps fifteen minutes, I held my wound as tightly as I could, telling myself to breathe, keep awake and not give in to the overwhelming sensation to faint. If I pass out, I joked, I'll die near a 7-Eleven, instead of in front of Grauman's Chinese Theater. Not this way! Not murdered by Hispanics, so many of whom I love.

Introduction

My Good Samaritan, unafraid, an avid Christian I'd later learn, Mike Bunnell, stopped, opened, but didn't shut his car door. He took me to the emergency room at Kaiser Hospital on Sunset Boulevard, just a few blocks from where I was stabbed. I was in for a long surgery to repair the sliced renal vein and left kidney—my recovery would be slow, one step at a time. It's a mystery such an unwanted event led to my sensing the inter-connectedness of the attackers, a hero who saved my life, the surgeons-nurses-therapists who healed me, police, friends, students, and family visiting me in the hospital: all coming together. This unexpected, difficult trauma angered me at times, but mostly I felt grateful to be alive and willing to forgive. As police showed me pictures of gang members, I noticed their resemblance to some of my students: dark, Latin, handsome, looking older, more hardened than their ages. You hurt me, *hermanos*, but I truly forgive you. I cannot like you, but I won't close my heart to you. I agree to cooperate with the police to find you, young men, who perpetrated a payback on the "wrong man." You need to face the consequences of your harmful actions. I could identify two of the six gang members, but the police gave up after a year of searching. No witnesses came forward.

I would later visit the doctors, therapists and nurses to thank them and give small gifts. A female therapist at Kaiser once asked, "Do you want to talk about it?" I just wept the entire hour with her; her warm, open, and understanding presence unearthed deeply buried tears. Without Mike's generosity, good luck, and the preparedness of expert medical care, I would not have survived.

On five occasions I spoke with police officers who visited during my hospitalization. They related that a different gang in the same week had stabbed an elderly man in the spine, taking his wallet and watch, the cruel act paralyzing him from the waist down.

Police expressed frustration with the huge gang problem in Los Angeles. We talked about the gangs from El Salvador, Mexico, Vietnam, East and South L.A. I told them about my Vietnamese, Salvadoran and Mexican students, and that I had attended funerals for some of them, who were murdered in drive-by shootings. We lamented the senseless loss of young people. I sadly remembered two untimely deaths at a facility in Baldwin Park where I taught: Francisco, a bright, promising, charismatic resident was found dead in the bathroom, a needle stuck in his vein for a heroin fix; and Lewis, a tall, thin, handsome Vietnam veteran was discovered one early gray morning hanging dead from a tree in the yard. Lewis was soft spoken and gentle, but haunted by the emotional, conscious and unconscious memories of war, "death's feast."

At times, our hospital/police business conversations meandered into our personal lives. I had never before felt close to police officers, nor had I thought much about how tough their jobs were, in often hostile surroundings. Here we were, officer and victim, interviewer and interviewee, engaged in police business yet also enjoying ourselves in our varied conversations, some humorous. At times, laughter hurt my stapled stomach. Sometimes I was groaning in pain from the after-effects of a long surgical wound, zippered together from my stomach to the bottom of my chest. Violence in my attackers, kindness of an ordinary hero, dedicated nurses and doctors, encouragement, thoughtfulness, connecting with caring police officers. All in all, I was a lucky man.

Consuming forty million tons of material per second to sustain us, the Sun is exploding as one of 400 billion stars in the Milky Way, swimming in the cosmic sea of 100 billion galaxies. We are small, yet of great value, with a precious opportunity to live our lives, in harmony and purpose with the stars, moon, sun and Earth intermingling, the whole vibrating mesh of life coursing through us in every breath.

****

Several Asian cultures believe humanity emerged from a bamboo stem. In the Philippine creation myth, legend tells that the first man and the first woman each emerged from split bamboo stems on an island created after the battle of the elemental forces (Sky and Ocean). In Malaysian legends a similar story includes a man who dreams of a beautiful woman while sleeping under a bamboo plant; he wakes up and breaks the bamboo stem, discovering the woman inside.
—Wikipedia: Bamboo

The preceding account relates to a time when my wounded body bent like a stalk of bamboo stretched almost to the breaking point. This event and lengthy recuperation provided me with a unique opportunity to reflect. Confined to a hospital bed, I spent time examining my role and effectiveness as a high-school and adult-school teacher. Experiencing violence at the hands of young people, I had to consider "what they didn't learn," and if they were even afforded the chance to study. I examined the quality of my teaching and the need for educational institutions to promote global and spiritual awareness to address violence and hostility, to treat others as we wish to be treated, the Golden Rule in its humanitarian and secular sense. After the sudden and brutal attack, I had to accept the ire inside. Anger is inevitable; it's how one responds to the anger that matters in our evolution as human beings, as I've experienced both in positive and negative ways. Anger, like greed and lust, is a strong energy, which can be used constructively rather than destructively. As I mature, I refrain more from hurting myself and others.

Teachers, parents and community members are collaborating to create a more peaceful and open classroom, extending to the world. The Internet-digital generation can, as generations before them, use the process of attaining a high-school education as a coming of age, growing into personal power and civil socializing. Some students apply themselves; others waste too much time. Some are polite; others sometimes disrespectful. Uninteresting, almost never.

I feel it as a sacred trust to teach the very different students who become a part of my life. I want them to give focused energy to their studies, and to take responsibility to make the lessons lively and suitable. I attempt to stimulate their curiosity. At times, during a group discussion a student might tell me to slow down; others seem to quickly grasp the material. Technology and modern teaching methods can accommodate our different learning paces. It's not necessary that all students learn the same material at the same time. I've had a few students who were too emotionally troubled to be pushed to study diligently. A teacher's patience can have a healing effect, and usually with time, the distracted student takes the first steps to study. I aspire for the students to progress academically at their own rhythm, and as behooves their teacher, to become better human beings.

****

Introduction

True education is an Inclination join'd with an Ability to serve Mankind, one's Country, Friends, and Family; which Ability . . . should indeed be the great Aim and End of all Learning.
—Benjamin Franklin

Given context through our stories and reflections, this collaborative book presents suggestions, but principally conversations of the heart and mind about the best education to prepare our children for both the known and the unforeseeable future. Educators are convinced that intellectual and emotional maturity go hand in hand. At a Christmas party, I snapped a picture of my niece Jenny and her boyfriend Chris, soon to graduate from UCLA. Earlier in the evening, Chris told me he was offered a high-paying job in the field of computer science. Full of satisfaction that his schooling paid off, and resolute to work, he was enthused by the intriguing opportunities available for those who train for the job market in our changing world.

Energized by promising discoveries about the brain's potential, aided by tools such as the Internet and the mobility of smartphones, we appreciate the wise use of technology. We are high-school students and parents, and an adult and high-school teacher who eight years ago found himself no longer instructing predominantly Latinos, but suddenly teaching mostly Asian students. Chinese adult students have shared concerns about their high-school children and the perplexing process of adapting to American schools. They lament how different it is in China, Taiwan, Vietnam, Thailand, Laos, Hong Kong, Indonesia, Malaysia and Cambodia. They complain that American classrooms overlook teaching moral concepts, unlike in the East where instruction includes Confucianism: morals, right and wrong, and the

Golden Rule. Such teachings allow the students to form empathy, a conscience based on learning to do good and avoid evil. A tradition of wisdom, Confucianism is not a religion. Since public schools in the United States are forbidden from teaching religion, the parents wonder how empathy and conscience are cultivated. How do US public schools teach character and moral development without violating the separation between church and state? Curious about differences, I sought to understand the concerns common to the Asian immigrant. I investigated Eastern education systems, learning about their wisdom (Confucianism, Buddhism, and Daoism), inventiveness, respectfulness, enthusiasm and practicality. I tried to incorporate the best of both worlds, taking these virtues from the East and including them in modern education. In the West we are perhaps stronger in the scientific understanding of the unconscious, and the brain's need for respite and refreshment to maximize collaboration, creativity and "thinking outside the box."

This conversation takes place in the San Gabriel Valley, which is relatively privileged, but not without problems that permeate society and its high-school education system as a whole. The business of education is tough and requires ongoing attention. In the Los Angeles Unified School District (LAUSD), fifty percent of teachers resign after working just five years. Superintendent John Deasy hopefully will be able to coordinate administrators, teachers, students, parents, union, and the business community to implement his vision of excellent schools for diverse communities. An op-ed piece by Coleen Bondy (*Los Angeles Times*, January 29, 2012), from Grover Cleveland High School in Reseda, California, relates some of the difficulties for schools in the LAUSD: family discord, drugs, disrespect of students/teachers, violence, lack of discipline in the classroom, and an absence of student interest and attention. Teachers from some high schools report witnessing violence. A teacher friend quotes Rodney King to his students, "Can we all get along?" At Coleen's high school, there are two full-time police officers and one probation officer, along with security personnel, to keep the peace for 3,800 students who attend crowded classes. She perseveres: "I work with an incredibly intelligent, caring, talented group of people. I also work with many brave, sweet, bright, extraordinary teens." On January 8, 1964 Lyndon Johnson announced a War on Poverty, which would result in a $947.5 million antipoverty bill to help more than thirty million citizens. In his State of the Union address, he emphasized improved education as a cornerstone of the program. Today likewise, motivated by our children's welfare, we are challenged to improve and democratize our education.

****

A person cannot teach another person directly;
a person can only facilitate another's learning.
—Carl Rogers, *Freedom to Learn*, 1969

I started teaching as an enthusiastic twenty-four-year-old at an all-boys private school, Bellarmine Prep in San Jose, California (1969–1971). My first year was a disaster. Wanting to please in order to be accepted, I often lost control of the class. I was overly accommodating to the teens' propensity for fun rather than attentiveness. I organized lessons well but did not prepare myself emotionally and socially. Overly proud, I never asked for help. Although I enjoyed coaching basketball, as the end of my first year approached I no longer wished to be a teacher. Six weeks before the end of my first year, the principal, Francisco Gonzaga, asked me to drop by his office. An efficient and fair administrator, he was a tall, slightly overweight, ruddy-faced, down-to-earth man who liked playing three-on-three basketball with the students. "You're doing well as a basketball coach but miserably as a high school teacher. Your team raves about you, but your students criticize you. Apply your coaching skills and strengths to teaching your students in the classroom. Each class has a group dynamic, so establish a corresponding social and educational milieu conducive to learning. Don't be afraid to stand up for yourself."

I asked myself why I was a competent freshmen-sophomore coach and a failure as a classroom teacher. I concluded that, in contrast to my attitude toward students, I shared a passionate interest in basketball with the players. We were hands-on, executing drills and strategies, scrimmaging to prepare for the next contest. We felt excited because we were "learning and playing on the job," and relied on each other through thick and thin. At the end of one game, I made a terrible coaching error, which cost us the win. The opposing team, behind by one point, inbounded the ball from under their basket with two seconds left on the clock. Unfortunately, I didn't coach the players to pressure the inbound pass, but had my team fall back to mid-court to defend against a long pass and quick shot. The in-bounder rolled the ball to save time; the game clock starts when the ball is first touched. Of course, I should have shouted out to a player in a good position: "Steal the ball!" I can play it in my mind after all these years: the ball rolling close to mid-court, an opposing player sprinting to pick up the ball, one dribble and a mid-court heave as if the basketball were a baseball, swish, nothing but net, game over. The stunned players grumbled at me, but soon started to kid around and show their support. "Don't sweat it, Coach. Lucky shot." Red-faced, I apologized. We didn't have time to dwell on it, but "mental replays" kept me tossing and turning all night long.

In practice, we worked on basic skills such as blocking out, rebounding, passing, shooting lay-ups, jump shots, set shots, free throws, and offensive and defensive techniques. We implemented a smoothly choreographed weave offense, taught by the varsity coaches, including high and low screens, give and go, back door, fast breaks, and pick and rolls. I was lucky to have players who became adept at playing as a team, liked to have fun, exulted with wins, but didn't dwell on losses. The players were mostly good sports, but there were moments when tempers flared. In the gym, I was able to handle volatile situations, but in the classroom I was not. The varsity coaches taught us man-to-man and zone defense, and most importantly, when to switch from one to the other. I knew I was at the beginning level of coaching, but I mistakenly thought I was more than a novice in the classroom. I sat at the feet of the varsity coaches, and did my best to apply their instructions. Being associated with the players and coaches was an unexpected gift in my early troubled times as a teacher. Our players shared a youthful camaraderie, rooting for each other, eager and appreciative of the opportunity to play on the school basketball team. Could I possibly bring play *and* discipline to the classroom? Could I excite the students to be engaged in learning, some of it inevitably tedious, as some basketball drills and calisthenics can be?

Coaching was fun yet, when teaching an academic subject, I felt a huge knot in my stomach. After my colloquy with the principal, determined to grow as a teacher, I began the final weeks of the year. Soon I was to experience a "turnabout," but habits and emotional hang-ups don't die overnight. The students continued to be loud and disrespectful, and my presentations fell on deaf ears. Mark, a year younger, and also a first-year teacher, taught next door. One afternoon, I heard loud yelling coming from his classroom, so I opened his door and saw Mark standing frozen in front of his desk. Out of control, the students were throwing paper wads at each other, against the wall and finally at Mark. Livid, I screamed at the students. The classroom fell silent. All my repressed resentment was expressed in: "Enough!" My fair-skinned friend's face was a crimson red; he was too humiliated to call the office. Not wanting to encounter his students again, he quit that afternoon. Seeing myself in my friend, standing helpless and mortified in front of his class, I had to accept that, to an important degree, we teachers determine how we are treated by our students. During the rest of the week, I developed a steely stare rooted in the memory of my buddy, without caring if I was liked or not. Silenced by my righteous anger and knowing Mark quit because of mental stress, the students realized the cruelty in their fun, and began to respond in the final weeks of the school year. My students and I learned that mutual respect, based in self-esteem, is hard-earned. I appreciated that, just as being a coach is a privilege and opportunity, teaching was likewise a gift and a responsibility. I found I could make demands on my students.

Learning from other teachers and literature, I discovered that stimulating interest, curiosity, and a love for learning in the students is an essential part of teaching. In a video interview, Bill Moyers talked with Isaac Asimov, author of *The Roving Mind*; Asimov spoke of the "power of curiosity" and our obligation as educators to teach creativity, based in freedom of thought and expression. Parents and teachers likewise want to encourage the special abilities and sensitivities of their children. Holding a PhD in chemistry, Asimov said he knew too much about chemistry to get excited about it. Wanting new knowledge, Asimov taught himself astronomy without ever taking a course. He wrote more books on astronomy than on any other subject. Asimov urged students to learn as much about the universe as they could, and enjoy it through the power of attraction and innate ability. We ideally educate ourselves in "what strikes our fancy," becoming "ferociously interested," and engaged in a challenging and enjoyable quest for knowledge. High-school students are usually only beginning to discover where their interests may lie.

I motivated the basketball team to play from the desire to do their best, and for the fun of it. I took my principal's counsel to encourage effort and a sense of individual and team satisfaction in the classroom as well as on the basketball court. The goal was the same: to nurture the undeveloped human potential within the unique student.

In a mostly calm and attentive atmosphere, during my second year, the students were inquisitive and studious. I wanted to be sure students' questions would not go unanswered. If I didn't know, I would research and consult with more experienced teachers. I saw more clearly the need for all of us to question, imagine, recognize what we know and what we don't, converse, and learn collaboratively in a civil and humorous manner. No longer intimidated by the students, I understood many of them overestimated what they knew, and that I had the obligation to stand up and teach. As we continued our education in earnest, the students and I talked more humbly about our abilities. I faced my emotional fears, which allowed the students to walk over me in the first year. Bad days were rare; there was an excited and eager vibration in the air. I welcomed discussion, disagreements, and suggestions. Correcting papers attentively and giving suggestions to the students led to rewarding conversations and an uptick in my confidence. Through our interactions, we appreciated how little we knew practically, emotionally and intellectually.

Finally, I engaged the process wholeheartedly and humbly at step one, embarking on a long, rewarding career in teaching.

During this turbulent era in American culture, torn apart over the war in Vietnam, I spent many of my weekends exploring the counter-culture with its music, activism, demonstrations, hippies, gurus, personal, artistic and social expression, and intellectual debate. Berkeley and San Francisco were magnets for me. It was the age of Be Here Now; Black Power and Oakland's armed Black Panthers; Women's Rights; César Chavez and the grape boycotts; Sal Castro and the weeklong walkout of students from Lincoln, Garfield, Belmont, Wilson and Roosevelt high schools to protest injustices in education for Latinos in Los Angeles; The Stonewall Inn riot and demonstrations in Manhattan giving birth to Gay Power; Oscar Romero of El Salvador and Liberation Theology with its Preference for the Poor; Native American Spirit-based religion; American Indian Rights; and the New Age Spiritual Supermarket. A dear friend and fellow teacher, half American Indian, tall broad-faced Leonard, asked me to volunteer with him and others; we collected clothes, blankets, food, and supplies for Native Americans who, on November 9, 1969 had occupied Alcatraz in scenic San Francisco Bay. They were on Alcatraz for seventeen months. The activists began to fight amongst themselves, "being their own worst enemies," said one of the organizing leaders. On June 11, 1971, one of the leaders was arrested for stealing copper from Alcatraz, and it was over. But the takeover of Alcatraz helped bring Native American concerns into mainstream awareness.

Teaching can be a sobering experience. I became more sensitive to the mystery of the unknown, and our small but real participation in the universe. I took to heart the aphorism of Austrian analytic philosopher, Ludwig Wittgenstein: "The rational mind only describes a tiny room in a vast cosmos and beyond this we cannot speak." I didn't have life figured out, but the hard work as a high-school teacher was paying off, and I knew I had found my occupation. Over the years, I have taught in college (Philosophy of Religion), high school, Adult Special Education, Basic Skills, GED, ESL, SAT and Mental Fitness in convalescent hospitals-hospices. I hope the reader might find accounts of these teaching experiences interesting. When I was attending Loyola High School, Los Angeles, from 1959 to 1962, teachers introduced me to fascinating worlds of literature, mathematics, science, history, politics, philosophy and religion. I had the chance to discover the areas of study that called to me. The engaging interplay between a teacher and student was life-changing, usually in a positive way. Teachers urged me to find solutions not only to academic problems but also to everyday struggles and profound personal questions. I was fortunate to have as models creative, funny and wise high-school teachers.

****

The eight chapters of *Bamboo Bending* combine a critical discussion of education with stories of students, parents, and my life as a teacher. Certain dramatic events shaped the person I am today. I identify myself with my work as a teacher and with the people in my life that I've loved. Chapter 1 reflects on the subject of high-school education in a predominantly Chinese community in the San Gabriel Valley. In discussing the Scholastic Aptitude Test (SAT) and varying topics, high-school students tell me about Tiger Moms, angry arguments, happy reconciliations, and their deep need to be listened to and appreciated for who they are. Chapter 2 summarizes scientific findings in neuroscience about the evolving teenage brain and its great capacity to encode knowledge and habituate abilities to survive, do well, and be happy. Analyzing and commenting on recent left-brain and right-brain studies, parts of this chapter stand out in their technical complexity. While left-brain dominant readers may enjoy such intricate science, some right-brainers may want to scan over them and go directly to passages related to teaching writing and balancing IQ and EQ. Chapter 3 reviews the findings of education's reformers, who are encouraging students to adapt and grow within a global, Internet-digital society by learning relevant cognitive, emotional, practical, innovative, and community-based skills. The chapter ends with an account of my volunteer service in southern Mexico. Chapter 4 discusses the creation of optimal study environments: the importance of positive emotional attitudes, diet, exercise, sleep, stress reduction, relaxation, focused attention and effort, and spiritual health. I relate my study-meditation with Chinese Buddhist friends and describe my work as a therapist and teacher at a mental health clinic in East Los Angeles. Chapter 5, through student interviews, shifts attention to Chinese high-school students' points of view. Here student is teacher. Chapter 6 interviews Chinese parents about their children's education in contrast with their own. Now parent is teacher. Chapter 7 discusses two controversial parents, Wolf Dad and Eagle Dad, and deliberates about topics based on Amy Chua's *The Battle Hymn of the Tiger Mother*. Do we consider the training of our children principally from a Pavlovian perspective or a humanistic one? I talk about teaching mental fitness in programs for seniors. Chapter 8 focuses on life-long learning, living creatively, and growing prosperously in the twenty-first century. I recount my experience with hospice.

Though *Bamboo Bending* highlights my teaching SAT to Chinese high-school students, I've taught and continue to teach students from various countries. Knowing a wide variety of people through teaching, I sense that human nature, though complex and difficult, is basically good and forgiving, and that we are happier when we treat others compassionately, just as we wish to be treated. For the most part, I've found it easy to see the beautiful, inner heart of my students, full of dynamic and unusual potential. Nothing, of course, about our human nature is so black and white; we all struggle with the darker sides of our personalities. We can exhibit heroic, loving kindness as well as give into the temptations of vice and deadening hatred.

When I was in high school, I was puzzled that Anne Frank who, in horrific circumstances in Holland, still affirmed, "No matter, I still believe that at heart man is good." As a Catholic, I held what I now see as a mistaken view. I was taught through Irish Catholic culture and religion, that people were born in original sin. I interpreted that emotionally to mean I was naturally bad and guilty. Some theologians I favor today, such as Matthew Fox, speak of original goodness. I will explain how Buddhist meditation and later contact with Chinese Buddhists have positively affected my spiritual life, while at the same time confirming my conviction for the ongoing need to be critical of clergy of any denomination who abuse followers or preach hate and discrimination.

Everything in our contemporary world is accelerating just as our universe, propelled by the antigravity of dark matter, is expanding rapidly into deep space. Despite the hastened unfolding of the cosmos, we humans are drawing closer to each other. Reformists are urging us to keep interconnecting our resources, and employ teaching methods adapted to the context in which we learn. We have come to realize the importance for each teen to be educated as a whole person, with a moral compass be it from religion, spirituality, civility, aesthetic sensibility, or secular humanism. Educators find that the cross-fertilization of wisdom from East and West can contribute to a successful educational system. It starts with respectfully listening to each other.

1

Listen

Brain research being done today reminds us of the relative importance of emotion over pure reason, social connections over individual choice, character over IQ, emergent, organic systems over linear, mechanistic ones, and the idea that we have multiple selves over the idea that we have a single self.
—David Brooks

Out of the blue, a panting high-school student approached as I was preparing a lesson. I would soon witness the transformation of an out-of-control babbling kid to one calm enough to have a conversation with, an example of the emotional rollercoaster many teens experience. "Just listen to me, Mr. Morgan," he blurted out. His bloodshot eyes bore evidence that he had been weeping. He was still a child, but more, he displayed a dramatic teenage need and urge to assert himself: anger mixed with extreme frustration, the kind that can lead teenagers to emotional breakdowns. He caught my complete and immediate attention. "Yeah, I'm here." His face was splotchy red as if he had been slapping himself in a fit of shame and rage. Hanging over his teenage complexion of "dreaded zits" was long stringy hair dangling in every direction. His head, at first bowed, jerked up and shook; he finally settled into rocking like a Tibetan monk chanting. At times overcome with tears, slowly he made eye contact. He related he had just fought bitterly with his mother about going to bed late. His mother felt he took too many breaks during his nighttime study. They lost their tempers and, emotionally hurt, said terrible things to one another. "You don't love me. You don't appreciate me. Why do you do this to me?" Mom demanded he skip evening breaks, except for dinner, and go to bed earlier. She then lost control and began screaming. Equally enraged, he stormed out, slamming the door so hard he broke it, surely disturbing the neighbors. He told me between gasps of air that his outburst was the result of pent-up anger. He said he was sorry, and that he hated himself. I knew the feeling.

I asked him to sit down and breathe. Words poured out as he gradually calmed down and began gesticulating. "I know what I'm doing, Mr. Morgan. I psych myself up, energize, and pace myself to complete homework assignments. My body clock doesn't match my mom's any more. I need breaks to watch an occasional TV show or get a snack, listen to music, walk around a while; then I can go back to study. There is too much pressure to get to bed by 11:00. I need some understanding and flexibility. I get all A's, but my mom screams anyway. It's still not good enough. I feel hopeless. What more does she want? She doesn't understand her method of studying is not natural for me, and that nagging doesn't help me study harder or faster. She needs to trust me." I listened, captivated by the raw emotion and candor of his story. Seeing the problem "out there"—with some perspective—helped my student compose himself. Luckily, it was the rare day I had all the time in the world. The son calmed down, and while feelings were hurt, I was happy that mom and son were intact.

Turning the tables, and still with great emotional intensity, he asked if I had ever made a "scene" from anger. The question threw me off; after all I was prepared to talk about *his* problem. However, my mind immediately transported me to another place and time, and appearing on my mind's silver screen, I replayed for the hundredth time losing the cherished job and coworkers I loved, when I, an adult, like the teenager in front of me, "lost it" to the demon of anger.

Listen

****

For only a few seconds measured in real time, but seeming like a full-length movie, uncomfortably I watched the scene from years ago, witnessing once again my wrath directed at the adversary, my boss, and the director of El Centro Community Health Center. We had weathered a long and brutal labor struggle we won, but which I just could not put behind me. As a bilingual recreation therapist and Special Education teacher in this City of Commerce mental health clinic, I, along with team members, provided support to emotionally challenged individuals suffering conditions such as depression, schizophrenia, anxiety, panic disorder, and drug/alcohol addiction. Client activities often included Daily Life Skills and Recreation (outings to the ocean, eating lunch in restaurants, bowling, outdoor games, visiting the zoo and parks) together with exercise, art, dance-movement, group therapy and anger management led by a psychiatrist or psychologist. We opened from 9:00 a.m. to 3:00 p.m. for our clients, conducted intakes, prepared classes and activities, meeting from 8:00 a.m. to 9:00 a.m. and from 3:00 p.m. to 5:00 p.m. to discuss our clients. Our team was composed of a team leader (PhD in Psychology), two Unit Leaders (one English-speaking, one Spanish-speaking), an RN, a community mental health worker, a psych tech, a secretary, three part-time psychiatrists, three recreation therapists, and a medical caseworker.

The East Los Angeles community welcomed us and gave the workers and clients perks such as discounted prices for lunch, a Christmas party, donated birthday cakes and most importantly made sure the at-risk population was understood, and allowed to mingle securely in the community. My work was demanding, fulfilling and interesting. I learned from in-services and the variety of experiences at the clinic. Welcomingly embraced and protected by the neighborhood, our clientele was 80% Hispanic, with more than half Spanish-speaking only.

I was attached to that job, and I lost it in a moment of uncontained anger. Carried away by buried emotions, at the very first staff meeting after the successful effort to establish a union—which for the first time elevated salaries to a dignified professional pay range—I vented my anger at the director. "Right On," fellow workers yelled; others were silent, frozen in shock. All the administrators, staff, doctors, psychiatrists, nurses and therapists were present for the director's talk just after the union contract. The atmosphere was tense. There were lingering adversarial feelings between the staff and administration; some of us on both sides were still seething. The battle was over—we had a victory—but my nerves were raw from the bitter fight. I should have been down at Venice Beach decompressing, but I was shaking my fist. We were victorious but I felt turbulence inside; I could not relax and return to the normal routine of work and civil discussion. I was carrying the past months' frustration with me at the meeting. The boss had done everything to block the union, but that was yesterday.

Both sides had recruited help from the community. It was nasty, even cruel at times. The principal organizers were targets. There were a half dozen on each side who, with their cronies, were intimidating. Neither side gave up easily. After recognizing the unwavering energy and dedication of the striking workers, the administration finally relented and agreed to the conditions of the union. We had put up a long fight and endured slashed tires and late night threatening phone calls. Our picket lines were vociferous: "Pay professional wages to the doctors, nurses, therapists, and all the staff. *Ahora*!" Picket signs with charts highlighted the contrasting administration pay/benefits (administrators set themselves up handsomely), but the staff's pay was dramatically low. Shared outrage and purpose brought the staff together. When on strike, we did fundraisers to help strikers with pressing needs. We were convinced of our cause to improve the worker's lot. Both staff and administration paid each other back with dirty tricks. The police were summoned at times to keep heads cool during the strike and, luckily, with the agreement of both sides, the police and security made it easy and as comfortable as possible for the clients to enter and leave the clinic. It was quite a scene, yet for the most part services were provided without major interruption. Notwithstanding the labor dispute, the administration and staff made sure the clients were taken care of.

****

Holding on to anger is like drinking poison
and expecting the other person to die.
—Buddha

My student relaxed, and we ended up hanging out and talking. He was able to put himself in his mother's shoes. He told me anger is always an issue, as many family members had bad tempers. This incident scared him. As he started to reflect, I could sense his distress was diminishing. He commented, "I never thought teachers get angry, especially you."

"Thanks," I said. "I'm old enough to be more peaceful. No matter how much we hide it from each other I think we each have our personal demons, which we must make peace with. Teachers need to keep learning just like everyone else."

He replied: "What do you do when you're boiling?"

"I found the commonsense advice of the ages in the words of a Vietnamese monk, Thich Nhat Hahn. 'Usually people lose themselves in a strong emotion and become overwhelmed.... In order not to become a victim, breathe and retain your calm, and you will experience the insight that an emotion is only an emotion, nothing more.... You do not try to forget your emotion; instead you try to be more of yourself, so that you are solid enough to deal with it.' Don't push away anger, but feel it without reacting, respond, put some space around it, don't be so victimized, redirect that energy. People have several methods, such as prayer and meditation, that they apply in their struggle with strong, sometimes destructive, emotions and actions. I take a time out to breathe; I'm often able to sense unmet needs behind the anger. I don't need to act out in a way that is hurtful; being hurt doesn't require hurting back. When I was in high school, a basketball coach told us breathing, emotion, concentration and rest need to work together for us to play skillfully. Breath and emotion are intimately connected. I find it helpful to practice conscious breathing when possible, perhaps taking ten full breaths while waiting in line or for a few minutes before I drive to a job or family gathering. I notice when I'm extremely off kilter emotionally, I need to walk or sit down and pay attention to thoughts and feelings that seem to pull me in different directions."

"So," the student said, "you're saying we don't need to keep the reactions from events alive; right now I feel my anger is not activated; I've slowed myself down to the point where I have self-control and can talk over the problem. Really, I'm OK, getting some perspective. Though not as dramatic as my breaking the front door, my mom and I have had arguments that lasted for a couple of days, because I just couldn't drop it, wanting to prove I was right. I'd slam my door shut several times for a full day; I could not help myself. I remind myself that we both have to compromise. I wonder about the condition of our front door. (*Laughing*) I wish I had more control *then*. Anyway, thinking about it, I know I should leave Mom alone tonight, just say hello, maybe a quick hug. We should give ourselves a break, don't dwell on it, don't add fire to what's making us mad, and be more patient with each other. Think about her as well as myself. Come to a practical compromise. I have to admit getting more organized has allowed me to get to bed earlier, which is what Mom wants. Yes, compromise, wherein both of us are important. I feel calm now but arguments are going to come up when Mom starts to nag. I need to get some resolution, peace. I don't want to explode like that again."

"If you push down hurt feelings long enough, they come out when least expected. We're maturing both intellectually and emotionally. People skills are important. Learning how to release stress positively is an essential skill for living. I know your mom will be happy to talk with you and listen to your side of the story. And you're right not to force that conversation. We all need a break from each other, so we can get back our sense of humor, right? 'Absence can make the heart grow fonder.' I like what you say about compromise. I agree with your mom that you should make the attempt to get enough sleep. I worry that many of my students do not get the sleep they need to fully rest and rejuvenate the connections between brain cells, vital for attention, concentration, memory, and executive functioning, as well as an overall sense of well-being."

****

Bamboo Bending

My only fixed truth is a belief in people,
a conviction that if people have the
opportunity to act freely and the power to
control their own destinies, they'll generally
reach the right decisions.
—Saul Alinsky, 1972

In 1970, I spent a sweaty summer in Chicago to train as a "Saul Alinsky" community organizer. Newt Gingrich, in his 2012 presidential campaign, mentioned Saul Alinsky in an inane attempt to suggest Newt's own political campaign was "American" but not Barack Obama's: "I am for the Declaration of Independence; he is for the writings of Saul Alinsky." I'm sure poor Saul Alinsky, "The Red," is shaking his fist from another realm of consciousness saying: "Of all people, why would I be against the Declaration of Independence?" Guru-founder of modern community organizing, author of *Reveille for Radicals* (1946), Chicagoan son of Russian Jewish immigrant parents, Saul Alinsky (1909–1972) was dedicated to improving housing and working conditions in poor communities such as Chicago's Back of the Yards neighborhood. "He wanted to see especially lower-income people who were getting pushed around to exercise some influence and even power over decisions that affected their lives" (Sanford Horwitt, former Washington Senior Congressional Aide, author of *Let Them Call Me Rebel: Saul Alinsky, His Life and Legacy*). Alinsky later devoted himself to training community organizers throughout the United States. Unlike Newt's insinuation, Alinsky advocated working within the system, as united communities with just causes, challenging and confronting the system to reform. Unlike the far-left, Saul said we should not aim to destroy capitalism. "It is necessary to begin where the world is if we are going to change it to what we think it should be. That means working in the system" (*Rules for Radicals*). Hilary Clinton wrote of Alinsky in

1969: "Much of what Alinsky professes does not sound 'radical.' ... His are the words used in our schools and churches, by our parents and their friends, by our peers. The difference is Alinsky really believes in them and recognizes the necessity of changing the present structures of our lives in order to realize them." Today less confrontational but still effective community organizing goes on in such institutions as PICO, started by Alinsky organizers and trainers, Juan Baumann and Jerry Helfrich. Both mentored me in Chicago. Juan, a personal hero, has dedicated forty years applying Alinsky principles in faith-based communities in the United States, El Salvador, Rwanda, Honduras, Guatemala, and Haiti.

****

During my training in Chicago, one of our teams organized apartment residents—mostly immigrants from Mexico and Central America who were living in slum conditions. The landlord procrastinated in the repair of lead-painted peeling walls, broken plumbing, and pest infestation. Some children suffered lead poisoning by ingesting paint chips from the walls. The strong conviction and united energy of the tenants provided the engine for us to form a base of solidarity: meetings, educational and artistic presentations, and social events such as potluck dinners and a dance with live music. The people were clear and emotionally positive, directed to achieve the objective of a cleaner and safer living environment for their children. Their cause was vital, pressing, just as innovative change for high school is. The residents had gone to the authorities, but their complaints were stuck in mountainous stacks of paperwork. I spent many hours going door to door, sometimes having it slammed in my face—*comunista!*—but meeting some remarkable people struggling to make it in America. Estrella

Chavez and Gilberto Chacon emerged as leaders. I also met some decent landlords who let me see their apartments, which were sparse, but clean, painted, and with working plumbing. A landlord told me, "I talk with my tenants. If I treat them well, they will respect where they live even if it's humble." These hands-on popular landlords were outraged that rat infestation would go uncorrected, but also could be critical of the organizers as being unfair to the landlord, who after all, promised to renovate at the beginning of the coming year. Though our protest was small scale, some of the sympathetic landlords asked us to forego creating "another protest with shouting, picket signs and exaggerated recriminations."

The 1968 Democratic Convention was fresh in the minds of Chicagoans. Americans watched TV scenes of police and National Guard beating yippies, hippies, students, assorted protesters, poets, and activists. In the summer of 1970, protests, especially against the Vietnam War, spread throughout Chicago and many US cities. Our venture was a needle in the haystack of discontent with the system, but it was still worthwhile because it was generated from a determined community. Late into the night, the animated organizers from various projects in the Alinsky training would meet to talk about projects and to get ideas and information. Soft-spoken Juan Baumann was one of the toughest and most practical mentors one could have. Estrella, Gilberto and the residents appreciated and employed some of Juan's crafty tactics.

A community developed around a cause based in human need: all people cherish a safe, clean home. Estrella and Gilberto organized through upbeat social networking within the immediate community. Saul Alinsky writes, "A good tactic is one the people enjoy." He used the phrase, "having a ball." Both the landlord and most of the Latino tenants were Catholic. The residents threatened the landlord: "Should you refuse, we'll make the long bus trip to your suburban church armed with photographs of the slum conditions." The landlord thought fellow Catholics would not embarrass him; he sent a notice that he was in compliance with city ordinances. He had received no orders to fix his buildings, because the inspectors were so behind schedule. He planned to repaint and fumigate the building in the new year, and insisted that it was the parents' responsibility to keep their children from eating paint.

Estrella and Gilberto met with the community to organize a fund-raising dinner-dance. A Catholic church let us use its large hall and kitchen; one of the volunteer's brothers was in a terrific Mexican band, which for one night rocked the group of tenants, families, community members and invited guests. A few Catholic seminarians and a diocesan priest joined us: *tacos de carne asada*, rice and beans, copious *cerveza*, conversing, flirting, dancing, electric music, mischievous kids running around. Leaders formulated a plan, which the residents would later discuss and approve: use the fundraising money to charter a large bus to travel to the landlord's suburban church for a peaceful but strong protest. We were confident we could bring the landlord to the bargaining table, but we had to play hardball. The tenants were ready to picket; we made large displays of photographs of the abysmal conditions of the apartments. We had copies of lead-poisoning medical reports blown up. Artists drew ordinary people—beautiful people—living in deplorable conditions. The tenants would picket at the time the landlord usually attended Sunday mass. We intended to embarrass the landlord in his own neighborhood. It was a disagreeable thing to do, but our issue of timeliness warranted it. Our bus of residents and supporters arrived as a morning Mass was about to end. Though the landlord didn't go to Mass that Sunday, several who were at Mass talked with the picketers, and there was lots of co-mingling. One of the priests asked the picketers, "What's the meaning of another protest?"

"Check out our pictures and reports of lead-poisoning from doctors."

"That's not right. Are you sure the landlord is aware of these conditions? What's the landlord's plan? I'll call him. Good luck; we're with you. Do your best to mediate the problem with the owners."

The following Wednesday, with the help of a pro bono lawyer, the tenants presented the landlord with a legal agreement to fumigate, paint, and fix the apartments. The landlord reluctantly signed and shook hands with the organizers but was still upset that he had been exposed at his church "without any defense against a busload of complaint." Had he forgotten our warning? One of the organizers reassured him: "Don't worry, in the church, we're disposed to forgive one another."

****

The same boss at El Centro Community Health Center who had given the union such a harsh time fired me forty-five minutes after my rant calling him every dirty name in the book. Though I was terribly distraught for a few months after being terminated, I am most grateful for the opportunity to have collaborated with some remarkable people, including administrators, therapists, psychiatrists, medical social workers and an office staff that kept the place running and laughing. I used my Alinsky training to play a small but real part in securing a unionized mental health clinic in East Los Angeles. No one knew the strike would take so long. It was pretty tough. First, there was the process to form a solid union and to then walk out and picket; the administrators' stubbornness almost broke the strikers' backs. Some

twelfth place. I summoned a burst of energy to pass the leaders one by one, as if in a slow motion movie. The school yearbook sports department put my crossing-the-finish-line-first picture in the yearbook; winning the race was one of the least likely things to happen to me in high-school sports.

We're sometimes too harsh with ourselves and our children. Priscilla, a thin, bright-eyed junior colored her hair in variations of pink-green-white, and wore tattoos and body piercing jewelry. At first, the family disapproved and would yell at her for disgracing the family. To the family's credit, with calm mediation and talking together, they accepted the daughter's freedom of personal expression. Priscilla explained: "My body tattoos are aesthetically pleasing to me. We're in high school; we experiment. I like some wildness and fashionable enjoyment of my body." The parents realized it's important to pick battles and add a sense of humor and perspective about everything else. We think we can control what happens, but in reality we are only part of the equation. This can be especially true in education. There's an old story of a man galloping on his fine stallion. As he passes a friend on the road, the friend shouts, "Where are you going?" Glancing over his shoulder, the rider yells back: "I have no idea where I'm going; ask the horse."

I've had students tell me how unfair it seems that another student whose work was inferior to theirs received higher grades on their essays. In *The Drunkard's Walk, How Randomness Rules Our Lives*, eminent author Leonard Mlodinow confesses that, under unusual circumstances, he wrote a paper for his 15-year-old son: "OK, shame on me. In my defense I should point out that I would normally no sooner write Alexei's essays than take a foot to the chin for him in his kung fu class. . . . Being a relentless rewriter, I gradually found myself sucked in, rearranging this and rewriting that, and before I finished, not only had he fallen asleep, but I had made the essay my own. . . . He handed me the graded paper: 'Not bad, a 93 is really more of an A- than an A, but it was late and I'm sure if you were more awake, you would have done better.' I was not happy." On a few occasions, I've witnessed moms and dads yell at their children because A– was unacceptable. Such moms and dads foist unwarranted pressure on their children; I've seen children tightening their bodies as parents castigated them for not achieving A's. If we step back from the situation, we realize that as important as effort and preparation are, they do not guarantee results. I've discovered that some teachers bypass the responsibility to actually read the essays they grade. Modern parents are realizing that achieving A's is not completely in the hands of the student, so they don't feel compelled to give their children the message, "You're not good enough if you don't receive an A." Rather they communicate and encourage the importance of doing one's best, enjoying the process of learning, and accepting appropriate demands for responsibility. Mlodinow explains: "A grade is not a description of an essay's degree of quality but rather a *measurement* of it. . . . In the case of the essay the measurement apparatus was the teacher, and a teacher's assessment, like any measurement, is susceptible to random variance and error." Most people who speak of successes acknowledge good fortune, along with the hard work.

****

How could I find out if there was more behind an argument between a mother and her son than just the inevitable, but sporadic, outbursts we have in our modern family lives? Together, the son and I formulated a strategy of bamboo bending. The son promised to compromise when he and Mom were calm. We discussed the sensitive balance between the pressure to study "Mom's way" and his need for short breaks and entertainment-play. He wished to feel free to finish his homework even if it was late. We talked about organizing his study space and materials, making the best use of the Internet, having files for each of his subjects, and scheduling by assessing what needed to be done, including SAT study. Confident that Mom would be receptive to him at home, my student—this marvel of teenage resilience—stood straight, exhaled deeply, and said goodbye. We both laughed when he blurted out that he was slightly worried that Mom might be enraged over the front door being yanked off its hinges. *Slightly?*

Teachers need to be sensitive to different cultural attitudes regarding education, taking from each culture its best qualities, and discarding strategies which do not work in America. Most of my students who arrive in the United States from Asia are very enthused about studying, which is a welcome quality, but doesn't always last if not nurtured. Taking into account the varying needs and capabilities of the students, I connect SAT study with skills the students need to be successful global citizens. I teach writing, critical reading, grammar, vocabulary, and at the same time, make the students aware of skills such as analyzing, imagining, empathizing, problem-solving and collaborating, abilities needed to survive in our globally instantaneously connected world. Students who master the SAT are adept at eight core reasoning skills: "mapping problems, analyzing problems, finding patterns, simplifying problems, connecting to knowledge, considering alternatives, thinking logically, and checking their work" (*McGraw-Hill's SAT*). If students join an SAT class, they likewise learn social skills and collaboration to support each other's study. I focus on the academic, but within the emotional context in which the student is learning at home and school. Every student has his or her rhythm, strengths, and weaknesses in modes of learning. The artistic part of being a teacher is to create a well-paced curriculum that facilitates the best learning possible for the individual student.

****

If there is divine creativity,
surely it is active in this inner soulsphere,
where brain matter produces emotion,
where love rewires the neurons.
—David Brooks

Many agree with Freud that what matters in life are satisfying work and love experiences. *New York Times* Medical Science and Health editor, author of *The Primal Teen*, Barbara Strauch interviewed research scientist Marian Damond about her pioneering work explaining how experience molds brains. A theme of this book is that we can change our brains/minds by promoting neural growth. We are able to influence the rewiring and strengthening of the synapses, the pathways within the brain. Developing new neurons and establishing additional connections influence our neural wiring and functioning for better or worse. Cultivating knowledge and emotional health, parents, business persons and high-school students are creating favorable experiences/environments for optimal learning and character-social emotional growth. Strauch talks about experiments showing how animal brains can grow according to the experience provided. In 1949, neuroscientist Donald Hebb, working at the Montreal Neurological Institute, decided to bring his children's pet rats to work. Hebb not only let his children keep rats as pets, but the rats ran all over the house as well. On a whim, Hebb put the pet rats in mazes used for laboratory rats. To his great surprise, the pet rats ran the mazes much faster. "Could it be," he thought, "that careening around the varied and unpredictable environment of a human house had somehow made the pet rats smarter, had made their tiny brains grow?" Student learning environments paradoxically need both order/organization and unpredictable risk-taking situations where students must apply insufficient knowledge to new learning tasks. With technology and imagination, the teacher can adapt to the way students learn and to what is important to be learned, including meta-skills such as critical thinking and imagining.

****

Staying in balance with the fluctuating waves of life is an ongoing process. Jonah Lehrer, Angeleno and author of *Proust Was a Neuroscientist*, says it well: "To fully understand the brain's mysteries, you can't impose some simple model. The brain tends to complicate things. It's not going to give us neat answers that conform to something we already believe. One mistake we make in thinking about creativity is that it's all or nothing, that you're Bob Dylan and Picasso or the rest of us. . . . Creativity is more universal. The type of creativity depends on the type of problem we're trying to solve." Scientist Bill Greenough researches the connection between experience and brain growth. "Think about the tasks of an adolescent and a child. They're developing social coordination and language capacity and cognitive function." The teen's prefrontal region of the brain must grow to accommodate an influx of information and pathways between that knowledge. The dominant prefrontal cortex influences one's psychobiological "self-control" executive ability to delay gratification. While the brain is appropriating new abilities, it also is losing some proficiency "such as the ability to learn a new language without an accent." Educators have long promoted the benefits of exposing young children to multiple languages.

Students can learn to focus, especially with good coaching and relevant resources. Teens access the prefrontal cortex's cognitive ability to voluntarily stop behavior as contrasted with just reacting. We hear the comment, "He's a perpetual adolescent," meaning he doesn't control himself but is irresponsibly controlled by impulses. The Antisaccade Task is one way that scientists measure impulse control. Scientists track the subjects' eye movements (saccades) while they are viewing blank screens. A light is projected passing through the screen. The subject is told to look in the opposite direction of the light; his ability to look away measures how well his brain controls impulse. We can play a principal part in the training of our brains to control impulses, be less easily distracted, improve the ability to attend to the task at hand, and become interested in the present.

****

Small is the number of people
that see with their own eyes
and feel with their own hearts.
—Albert Einstein

One way of controlling and integrating our impulses is through meditation, a practice that has gained acceptance in the West. I became familiar with Buddhist meditation through Japanese Zen teachers who came to California and taught many sore-kneed Westerners to "just sit." We paid attention to our breathing, physical sensations, thoughts, and feelings—being present to whatever was arising—and if we lost attention, we'd center ourselves in our breathing bellies. We might loosen an otherwise unrecognized tightened jaw or tense neck and shoulders. The meditator observes himself without reacting to impulses (such as wanting to punch someone after a thought of feeling hurt) while being aware of the body, a state exemplified in the following Daoist meditation, which my friend Michael Saso posted on Facebook. "The place to 'meditate' for 'enlightenment' is the belly, i.e. the body's center of gravity, not the will-desire or mind-judgment. The head, for thinking and judging, must be emptied to see the Dao, and the heart, for loving, must be freed from selfish desire to have true compassion. Inner emptiness meditation is to send the mind and heart into the belly, and burn them there like an alchemical furnace, so nothing is left, not even the ashes."

A skillful meditator develops the ability to focus and relax despite external distractions. There are myriad ways, adapted to the individual to deal with mental and physical stress. A businesswoman has a breakneck schedule, preparing to present final copies of extensive business plans, which she has meticulously edited. She explained her way to meditate. "What I'll do is envision myself in a round room; usually the walls are made of wood. My files of new business plans are trying to sneak between the door floors and between the walls. Someone's pushing more and more files through the opening to the room. I get a broom and just start sweeping them away. (*Laughing*) The guy's pushing in the files, running outside the walls, coming at me from all directions. So I quickly get to the point of attack and repel the stacks of paperwork. I clean my brain. I have so much work to do my thoughts sometimes won't let me alone, so I just keep sweeping the bothersome pressure out the door, out of my brain." Another friend said he relieved stress by sitting quietly outside in nature, and letting his mind have a life of its own to wander where it willed. "I take a break from thinking and reacting and find myself to be fully in my body, in a state sometimes free of thoughts wherein I feel inner peace, no separation between me and the world." There are meditation classes where leaders give instructions such as "Feel your stomach expand as you breathe in, contract as you breathe out. Pay attention to the belly expanding, filling, and the stomach contracting while exhaling. If your mind wanders, bring your attention back to your breath." Teacher Mark Coleman talks about the many styles of creating meditative states. "Sitting. Stillness. Movement. Yoga, tai chi, chi gong. Ones that cultivate the heart, mind and awareness and clarity, concentration meditation, new age meditations that focus on energy. Once you choose, you have to give it some period of time to evaluate."

Dr. Andrew Weil reported the findings of a study from Heriot-Watt University in Edinburgh, which concluded that, for some, the brain enters a meditative state when one is in the "green space" of nature. Mobile electroencephalography tracked the emotions of twelve people (admittedly a small sample) as they walked for twenty-five minutes through green spaces in the city which proved helpful for some of them to be more relaxed, present, and composed. Many of us can attest to the calming effect of being in nature, at the ocean, desert, mountain, a walk outdoors. I remember when a high-school senior camping out with Tom McGrath in the magical beauty of Yosemite in the heart of California: breathtaking, half-mile deep Yosemite Valley; powerful granite cliffs; sheer Half Dome; masterful rock sculptures; tall waterfalls along the Mist Trail; the pristine beauty of Tuolumne Meadows with brightly-colored flowers; and the giant Sequoias, Sierra redwoods of Mariposa Grove reaching high into azure skies. I recall watching the bears rummage through the garbage dump from the safety of our car; swimming in the lake, pools, and swimming holes; and cooling ourselves and our beers in cold rushing streams. I still hear the conversations of two young dreamers, feeling free, buddies under nights of dazzling "touchable" stars, usually hidden from us in smoggy L.A.

The English word "meditation" derives from Greek (*medesthai*) "to think" and Latin (*mederi*), a root meaning "to cure," also the origin for the English word "medicine." That seeming coincidence was not lost on Dr. Jon Kabat-Zinn, a pioneer who brought mindfulness meditation into mainstream medicine. Kabat-Zinn teaches a form of meditation called MBSR (Mindfulness Based Stress Reduction). Author of *Mindfulness for Beginners: Reclaiming the Present Moment—and your life*, Kabat-Zinn trained the US Olympic Rowing Team in 1984. "They compete sitting down and going backwards; they must stay in synch physically and mentally. Doing and being are intimately connected." In moments of stillness, silence, and non-doing, one gives up wanting anything else to happen. Drop into being; make friends with your mind. Come to your senses. Feel yourself breathing. Awareness is always available. According to Buddha, "The secret for both mind and body is not to mourn the past, worry about the future, or anticipate troubles but to live in the present moment wisely and earnestly." We come to be open to the known and the unknown of life, practice more common sense, and accept the mystery and element of randomness in our lives. Sitting with dignity and good posture, we ride the waves of our breath, in and out, unforced, allowing any thought, reverie, or emotion to arise and pass away.

Impulse control is a major problem for many of America's 2,193,798 prison inmates. In 1973, Bo and Sita Lozoff and Ram Dass began the Prison-Ashram Project, a service to prisoners wishing to do spiritual practices, thus transforming the jailhouse into an *ashram*, Sanskrit for "House of God," using the tough environment to grow spiritually and emotionally, making the jailhouse a monastery. In another program, experimental courses in meditation were given to inmates in 1997 at North Rehabilitation Facility in King County, Washington, and in 2002 in Bessemer, Alabama, at W.E. Donaldson Correctional Facility, nicknamed the "House of Pain." Inmates participated in ten-day experiments, with ten hours of meditation as voluntary rehabilitation. Based on the successes of these experiments, similar prison ten-day meditation classes were begun in California, Alabama, Massachusetts, Texas, Vermont, Taiwan, Israel, New Zealand, the U.K., and Mexico. The 1997 documentary, *Doing Time, Doing Vipassana* describes a significant prison experiment, the ten-day Vipassana meditation course given in Tihar, New Delhi's largest jail. "The students learn to observe their breath—by focusing on breathing at the nostrils—for the first three days. In doing this simple—yet difficult—task, the mind starts to become more concentrated and quiet. The student calms down. This is the first step in learning how to have control over the mind. On the fourth day, students learn to observe sensations in/on the body— such as heat and cold, pain or tingling, itching or even numbness and to try not to react to them; this simple attitude of non-reaction begins to change the habits of the mind" (Rebecca Shepard, *Intimate Meanderings*).

For the past five years, Ray Leonardini, author of *Finding God Within: Contemplative Prayer for Prisoners*, has been embarking on vital work: in a non-sectarian way, giving prisoners a method of twenty-minute, once-or-twice-a-day contemplative prayer. Ray directs the Prison Contemplative Fellowship, consisting of former and current prisoners who reach out to inmates and their families. A member of this brotherhood and sisterhood writes: "Centering Prayer allows me to deal with all those events and memories that I have chosen to avoid, especially the painful and shameful ones. I find as I deal with them, little by little, they lose their power over me." Inspired by models from the Christian contemplative tradition, such as Thomas Merton, Gerald May, and Ignatius Loyola, Ray studies, learns, practices, and teaches. "We are all prisoners in one form or another and some of us are behind bars." One does not have to be a Christian or a member of a particular religious faith to contemplate, to explore within, let go of thoughts and feelings, listen, and be quiet. "Our inner life is deeply our own, difficult to know, and hard to talk about. . . . We may choose a word, a simple word of one or two syllables, our 'sacred word,' not in a religious way, nor like a mantra used as a concentration technique, but sacred in its meaning to us. . . . Some prefer breath, life, yes, mercy, or any word that helps us to let go of our thoughts. . . . When thoughts begin to come, we just repeat our sacred word silently a few times and let the thoughts go by . . . move into the self that opens to Presence deep within. . . . Our 'knowing' is in the gut, not the head."

Meditation, inner exploration of the body-mind, has been around for centuries, predating ancient Buddhism and practiced by several traditions such as contemplative Christians and Kabalists of the 12th and 13th century. Scientific studies continue to uncover the brain's inner workings, and the ways the unconscious influences the mind. Paying attention produces longer telomeres, the DNA-based caps that insulate the ends of chromosomes, increasing longevity (*Clinical Psychological Science*, January 2013, Vol. 1, No. 1, 75-83). The meditator may sit quietly and alertly, allowing non-judgmental awareness of whatever is "inside."

****

Scientists studied the teen brain in a 2001 University of Pittsburgh functional magnetic resonance imaging (fMRI) research project. The maturing prefrontal cortex is the product of brain cell branches' overproduction, synaptic pruning (deactivation), and frantic "last moment" organization. In similar experiments, scientists study images of brain changes, which map the maturity and organization the brain needs to function optimally. We see our world through our conscious and unconscious brain-minds, affecting the way we learn and teach. In *Subliminal,* Leonard Mlodinow demonstrates the remarkable power of the brain and its ability to create the world in which we live. An experiment is conducted using an fMRI (measuring the blood flow in the brain and mapping it in three dimensions), to collect data from the brain to reconstruct an image of what a person is looking at, be it a bridge or a group of people singing. Reading the electromagnetic pictures of the brain without any reference to what the person is viewing, "the computer puts data from areas of the brain that respond to particular regions in a person's field of vision together with data from other parts of the brain that respond to different themes. A computer then sorted through a database of six million images and picked the one that best corresponded to those readings with amazing accuracy." Understanding how the brain operates and influences human interaction is called "social neuroscience." Though propelled by our genes, we can contribute, through experience and environment, to the cultivation of new connections in our brains, developing cognitive skills and mental capacities. We participate in the evolution of our brains.

As I've become more sensitive to the underlying emotional context within the unconscious, I've become freer from rigid expectations, and can adapt to the individual student with more understanding and humility. The teen's emotional life is similar to that of David Brooks' high-school character, Harold. "Harold's high school was structured like a brain.

There was an executive function—in this case, the principal and the rest of the administrators—who operated under the illusion that they ran the school. But down below, amidst the lockers and in the hallways, the real work of the organism took place— the exchange of notes, saliva, crushes, rejections, friendships, feuds, and gossip. There were about 1,000 students and therefore roughly 1,000 X 1,000 relationships, the real substance of high-school life." Brooks continues: "The study of conscious mind highlights the importance of reason and analysis; study of the unconscious mind highlights the importance of passions and perception. If outer mind highlights the power of the individual, the inner mind highlights the power of relationships and the invisible bonds between people ... the central evolutionary truth is that the unconscious matters most. The central humanistic truth is that the conscious mind can influence the unconscious." The challenge of teachers, administrators, and parents is to connect intelligence, passion and empathy to education. David Brooks' fictional teacher, Ms. Taylor, considers her students unique and complicated individuals, not just "mechanical receptacles" to fill with information, but real people. Learning flourishes in a climate of respect and mutuality. As the capacity for critical thinking skills increases in the teen, teachers and parents have to take into account that teen emotional sensitivity (fueled by "hormone hurricanes") can be intense, making a rocky emotional climate for education and family life, but also a potentially fruitful one.

****

Bamboo Bending

In less than two hundred years, we have
moved from a closed, static, hierarchical
universe of absolute space and time to an open,
dynamic, evolutionary, 13.7 billion year old
universe of relative space-time; from
analytical causal systems to contextual open
systems; from order and equilibrium to chaos
and non-linear systems; from cause and effect
to quantum entanglement. Added to these
scientific achievements is the ascent of various
technologies including artificial intelligence,
robotics, synthetic biology and nanotechnology.
—Ilia Delio

I'm optimistic but I also worry. We are only beginning to understand and respond practically to an inter-connected, changing and unpredictable world. Witness Dennis Rodman, former NBA super-rebounder, watching a basketball game in Pyongyang with young North Korean dictator, Kim Jong Un. Rodman calls Un a "normal guy." Most Americans see Un as far from normal in his actions. They went together to a nightclub with an all-girl band, and Rodman adds, "We were definitely getting down." Who'd have thought such an absurd meeting would occur? We're evolving and in process, alive and adapting, growing to match unexpected challenges, not static, not wed to the expectations of strict ideology but to the exigencies of our chaotic times.

Where will the money for education come from? Business and parent associations have to fill the budgetary gap, as well as advise and collaborate with the high school. Fixing our schools entails creating an effective and complementary alliance of students, parents, community members, and entrepreneurs. As an educator for many years in the San Gabriel Valley, I've met and learned from very creative high-school and adult-school teachers. Some of them are ineffective, but that's the exception to the rule. Parents need to stay involved with their children's schools and establish dialogue with teachers. Money can't be an excuse for non-involvement. In 2013 California, education continues to lose funding; we must reform our schools with fewer tax dollars. LAUSD spreads across 710 square miles, and is entrusted with 664,000 students. The future of US public education depends on expanding the network of support from parents and businesses in instilling skills needed in the global, technologically-advanced workplace. Our future depends on it. My students ask me: "When I graduate and go to college, will I be able to find a good job?"

In California, teachers are asked to develop good test-takers, which is fine and necessary, but standardized tests can be overemphasized. Some school administrators pressure teachers for high standardized scores, often neglecting the importance of other skills, such as using imagination to adapt knowledge to varying situations. Teachers must prepare for tests as well as teach skills such as flexibility of thought, ability to think quicker, verbal and written fluency, processing information from sensory input, making a good argument, expounding meaning, and problem solving. Feeling stressed about testing and inflexible expectations, some teachers forget teaching is creative and fun, along with the hard work. Since learning is a mutual and communal process, teachers grow along with their students.

Albert Einstein encouraged teachers to absorb their subject so they could present it clearly: "If you can't explain it to a six-year-old, you don't understand it yourself." Einstein's model of a curved, trampoline-like universe expands into vast darkness. Contemplating the great mysteries of life, we are like children "standing awestruck in a giant library with thousands of books in many languages." From a mystical sense of life and humility before the unknown, Einstein was able to create theories of physics. On a field trip to Griffith

Park Observatory, one of my students remarked: "I had a sense of wonder, which really took me out of myself. I felt we cannot totally know, but there is some togetherness, a unity of all the galaxies; I want to learn more about what I can never know completely."

Continuing to study, reflect and converse, I am less compelled to say I know the answers to the perplexing questions of life and death. Einstein's sensibility translated into his deep thirst for knowledge, which, along with devoted and focused "damn hard" work, included fun and relaxation, family and friends. According to Einstein, "Creativity is the residue of time wasted." Educators encourage their students to both concentrate on studies and take relaxing breaks as creativity emerges from focused attention as well as integration, gestating in the unconscious.

Like many of today's students involved in current affairs and global citizenship, Einstein's passionate activism against anti-Semitism illustrates the need to include empathy as an essential part of a Western liberal education. Walter Isaacson writes: "In retrospect, the rise of the Nazis created a fundamental moral challenge for America. At the time, however, this was not so clear. That was especially true in Princeton, which was a conservative town, and at its university, which harbored a surprising number of students who shared the amorphous anti-Semitic attitude found among some in their social class. A survey of incoming freshmen in 1938 produced a result that is now astonishing, and should have been back then as well: Adolf Hitler polled highest as the 'greatest living person.' Albert Einstein was second. Einstein wrote shortly after this poll in the popular weekly *Collier's*: 'The bond that has united the Jews for thousands of years and that unites them today is above all, the democratic ideal of social justice coupled with the ideal of mutual aid and tolerance among all men.'"

Listen

******

I agree with Yates that ideally education is the lighting of a fire, the desire and longing latent within the student to learn and continually hone the skills and meta-skills, to live a creative, loving and prosperous life. Igniting a fire in high-school students is an ongoing challenge and comes with relative success. Many teachers have shared the satisfaction of witnessing an enthusiastic student "getting it." Such moments may take the teacher by surprise as he or she is occupied with coaxing, surviving, presenting and organizing material, and challenging the student to study and discuss. There's a resistance to learning as well, including in myself. Once I had a small SAT English class, with not even one student wanting to study. They would do the minimum, needing constant reminders to focus on reading, writing, and grammar. Frustrated and concerned, and to the horror of the few teachers I told, I decided to pay each student a small monetary reward for completing a substantial number of quizzes, grammar and vocabulary exercises, critical reading, and SAT essays. I organized my classes well and let the students decide the order in which we completed the necessary work to prepare for the SAT test. I added a time when I asked trivia questions, concentrating on geography, as the students suggested. "You need to know about different countries, because in the future—as a global economy evolves—you may live and work in Europe, South America, Mexico, Asia, Africa, Central America, the Middle East, Australia, Israel, and other locations in which you may be doing business. You may marry someone from a different country." All the students completed the work and achieved good SAT scores; they promised they wouldn't tell a soul about "Mr. Morgan's bribery."

Many high-school teachers will tell you of difficult times with students who withdraw their energy from learning, and sometimes create distractions for other students. "I'm so bored." I tell my students that some are successful in learning a subject in university without a strong love of their material, but still study diligently, motivated to be in a particular profession. Some discover that the learning itself—even if the content is dull—can have a certain satisfaction. It's necessary in life to accomplish tasks that aren't instantaneously gratifying. Some former *reluctant* students become fulfilled professionals, and end up loving their work; others seem to be excited about life but not necessarily enthralled with their work. I see some students, even at their young age, reacting with wise perspective to highs and lows, the fluctuating currents of life. Others are anxious about what lies ahead. Unlike in my high-school days, a good number of students are anxious about employment, worrying that it's tough to find satisfying and well-paying jobs. Teachers encourage them not to give up and to be patient, to prepare well, but also enjoy being high-school students. Opportunities abound for those who are prepared to find them. I see teens happily making new connections and discoveries, excited by new experiences and thrills, along with suffering from boredom, depression, confusion, and worry about acceptance. Fascinated by challenges, students are impassioned about new possibilities, interested in making the world better, desiring to belong and even lead. Teens are national treasures, beautiful for sure, boy and girl no longer, man and woman not yet.

****

Listen

The solution to our economic and social challenges is the same: creating a viable and sustainable economy that creates good jobs without polluting the planet. And there is general agreement as to what that new economy must be based on.
One word: innovation ... we can develop the capacities of many more young people to be creative and entrepreneurial.
—Tony Wagner

When my stepson Jack was a boy, he loved inventing games. I was impressed by his creativity to conceive new and engaging play for his cousin Elena and other children. I saw in him a natural form of innovative intelligence, quickly able to imagine possibilities by making hand-made props for expressive play or engaging games. At the tender age of one and a half, Zoey—Jack's and his wife Bonnie's little girl—shows the same ingenuity to spontaneously devise her own ways of communicating and play. Tony Wagner, the innovation education director at Harvard's Technology and Entrepreneurship Center, is the author of *Creating Innovators: The Making of Young People Who Will Change the World.* Wagner writes: "Jobs of innovators and entrepreneurs will be immune to outsourcing or automation in the new global knowledge economy." The creative impulse is a natural drive to evolve, adapt, and grow, to imagine new ways to invent, communicate, work and play. Teachers are becoming better coaches by using state-of-the-art tools and experimenting with what works both intellectually and emotionally for the individual student, urging him or her to practice and study in a focused manner, take risks, solve problems, exercise passion, and cultivate a collaborative and civil spirit. Employers seek flexible workers who can execute not only long-term goals and strategies, but also improvise in response to changing circumstances. The manager communicates the basics of the job, but it is the worker who must create solutions when encountering problems. Conscious of the contemporary workplace, I remind my SAT students that focusing on the study material will not only be of great benefit for getting into an excellent college; it will more importantly improve attention, verbal fluency, memory, and collaborative-empathetic skills. These traits will transform the pupil and prepare him or her for the work world.

****

If America does not produce high imagination people, we are going to be a very poor country.
—Thomas Friedman

A female student, who had been in the United States for two years, told me: "In China, I followed my mother through every step of my education. Here we have to walk together. Before I only listened to her. Now we need to listen to each other. Sometimes my mother and father revert to treating me as if we were still in China. We argue but are getting to be better friends." I appreciated my student's determination to acclimate herself to a new world in America, while staying close to her family. For the ordinary student, the high-school experience is challenging, chaotic and difficult already. For the immigrant student, these challenges are magnified due to language and cultural adaptation. Not only must the immigrant student grasp complicated intellectual concepts, but he or she must survive in a new and foreign environment during this vital stage of physical and emotional growth.

Some parents tell me that it's critical for their child to attend a famous university. That's a wonderful aspiration; however, many children will not achieve straight A's and outstanding AP and SAT scores. I remind parents to be realistic and not to worry so much about the great university if it is not feasible. There are many notable colleges proficient at preparing students for the adult world. Teachers and counselors advise students about the importance of mentorship, working internships, and specialization. Each student has unique talents and inclinations that can be nurtured.

Employers want workers who adapt knowledge and talent by applying skills to changing conditions. Tony Wagner presents a helpful perspective for parents: "Admission into 'name brand' schools is more and more a matter of luck and no longer offers the competitive advantages it did 20 years ago. The push to get all A's distorts the purpose of school and distracts from acquiring the skills that will give kids a *real* competitive edge. To get into Harvard, Stanford, and Yale you learn to play a game, a game of perfect scores, building a resume, etc. The problem is, if you have not learned to collaborate, to take risks and learn from your mistakes, to create as opposed to consume—all qualities that matter in the world of innovation—then companies like Apple will have no use for you."

Many Asian parents and their children, most born in China, Vietnam, Cambodia or Taiwan, and some born as first generation Chinese-Americans, have become a part of my life. This book includes stories from my high-school English SAT class of Chinese students, and contains interviews with these students and their parents. The demographics of the San Gabriel Valley have changed dramatically in the past decade. The overwhelming minority had been Latinos, with whom I could speak in their mother tongue of Spanish. Now I teach mostly Asian students. In the classroom, this transformation was abundantly obvious.

¿Cómo estás? became *ni hao*; *gracias, xie xie* and *adiós, zijian*. The student body that once regaled me with savory empanadas, enchiladas, tacos, burritos, and mangoes now do so with moon cakes, *kung pao* chicken, dumplings, Asian pears, and red envelopes. Just as with my formerly predominantly Latino students, I find myself in love with the people, intrigued by differences in cultures and the opportunity to learn, teach and collaborate.

Teens have to deal with heightened emotional experiences, because their brains haven't fully developed. The teenage brain shows a remarkable period of transformation—the "most tumultuous" stage of a human's identity according to developmental psychologist, Erik Erickson. What is one's "ego identity," the sense of self that is acquired through stages of social interaction? Teens often find themselves in a limbo of uncertainly as to what they want. "I don't know *who* I am." Erickson postulates that the developmental struggle (physical, psychological, and social) for teens (age twelve to eighteen) is "identity versus role confusion." The teen may bemoan, "I don't know where I belong. How am I to manage school and societal demands? Before, my family took care of me; now I'm soon to be faced with my own decisions." Teens, with a confident sense of self, feel more independent and in control. In contrast, those unsure of their abilities, needs and desires feel less sure about themselves and the future.

Driven to explore possibilities, teens seek independence and expansion of relationships beyond home, which is still their basis of security and support. The parent has to be wise and understanding as the teenager bonds with peers. The world is calling, yet the teen more than ever needs a nourishing home to protect him from danger, while at the same time allowing freedom to fly. It's a time of developing emotional and social growth: a secure sense of self, verbal fluency, discriminative thinking, and a sense of direction by understanding what one wants. Teens experiment with different behaviors, activities, and roles. They may experience wild idealism as well as challenging lows. Are there ways parents can encourage their child to pursue his or her dream even when the parents have different goals for the child? Gabriel Jacobs tells a story about being a university student in the 1980s, when computer technology was exploding. Fascinated by the creative buzz of the growing technology, and the enthusiasm of his small group of friends studying computer science, Gabriel wanted in on the exciting scene. His friends were having fun creating new technologies and dreaming of future wealth. Gabriel's dad had another idea: Gabriel was to be a doctor. Though he did what his dad asked, he still had regrets. Some of his computer-tech university friends are now multi-millionaires. Gabriel is a successful, happy orthopedic surgeon, and says Dad was right in the sense of being practical, knowing his son would have a steady and lucrative career as a doctor. But Gabriel can't help thinking what could have been. As a parent, Gabriel says he listens to his kids' ambitions.

Listening and pondering the teenager's words is an efficacious start to comprehending the student mind. Understanding the subject of the next chapter—how the teenage brain learns, encodes and responds to stimuli—is essential in helping develop one's child mature into adulthood.

2

Encode

Teenagers can act like kids one day, adults the next, and have trouble overriding their impulses . . . adolescent behavior has a physical basis in the brain.
—Betty Ann Bowser

In some studies, fourteen-years-olds are less adept at recognizing other people's emotions than nine-year-olds. It takes a few more years of growth and stability before they finally catch up with their former selves.
—David Brooks

Willpower is trainable and cultivatable.
—Roy Baumeister

I gave up "fighting" with my high-school students. A few years ago, in a small classroom with seven SAT English students, among my noisiest and most distracted classes ever, I no longer felt the compulsion to change them. I ended a losing battle: forcing resistant students to pay attention. Rather I'd continue to use my imagination, prepare well, and provide the most favorable learning conditions, taking into account inevitable chaos and resistance. Still urging students to work diligently, I made my presentations more interesting by incorporating student energy to keep the class lively. I asked the students to shift their attention from extraneous impulses to the material at hand, and to notice when they were doing the lesson mechanically rather than truly comprehending. The students practiced concentration, memory, and verbal fluency games on the computer, as well as prepared for the SAT test. As they improved, they became fully engrossed in the exercises. I gave them a pep talk on the importance of SAT English, in particular expanding vocabulary and understanding it in context. We discussed a quote from E. D. Hirsch Jr., University of Virginia professor in Education and founder of Core Knowledge Foundation: "For guidance on what helps students finish college and earn more income, we should consider the SAT, whose power to predict graduation rates is well documented. The way to score well on the SAT—at least on the verbal SAT—is to know a large vocabulary.... There's a positive correlation between a student's vocabulary size in grade 12 and the likelihood that she will graduate from college, and her future level of income.... Vocabulary size is a convenient proxy for a whole range of educational attainments and abilities."

The students had a say in how the class proceeded and took turns leading group activities, and keeping us all on task. We made an agreement about what we were to accomplish, and decided on break times. A student made sure I knew he "hates school, but would experiment." We agreed to work quickly while checking for comprehension, inviting questions, and problem solving. The group energy carried the class, and I stopped over-teaching and feeling responsible for a successful outcome. Continuing to make sure up-to-date learning materials were available while prompting and coaching, I was surprised when a student announced: "No video games in class. Please pay attention. Do it, hey, stop talking; don't miss your chance. Let's go." I'm not always so successful with a difficult class, but such "turn-around" classes motivate me to never give up. Some students do love to study, as if they can't get enough, and even ask for homework, sending me papers to correct via e-mail. Like music to my ears, a student says she can't put down a novel she's reading for English. Others want to do the minimum, and can't wait until the class ends. *C'est la vie.*

****

> *I will do a flight of fantasy and work on some thinking, which is not thinking as you would understand it, but combinational play of some types of imageries and sensory feelings. Only when this activity comes to some resolution would I fumble in the other side of my head for words and for algebraic statements, which would permit me to communicate these insights to others.*
> —Albert Einstein

Einstein's description foreshadowed the future of the right-brain/left-brain paradigm. The architecture of the brain is a burning topic of scientific research and writing, and of course, class discussion. Scientists emphasize three principal capacities of the brain: learning (establishing-strengthening new connections), regulating (controlling oneself), and choosing (selecting). Ninety billion neurons, supported by one-hundred trillion synapses, each one firing from 5 to 50 times per second, create countless connections. The brain uses just as much energy when we sleep, and functions on three levels: brain stem reptilian (survival), limbic animal (emotional), and human cortex (thinking). A tormented student asked privately if the brain had the ability to change an inclination to commit a heinous act. "Am I a slave to my strong impulses? At least for now, I don't act out." I explained the brain optimally works as a whole, regulating, tempering thoughts and words, and controlling destructive actions emanating from anger, fear, lust, and greed. We all have our own forms of negative impulses; it's how we respond that matters. We don't have to follow impulses if we realize that they would be harmful to ourselves and others; we can grow in our ability to think before we act. Even if we may feel like "blowing our tops," we don't need to act out what we can rationally know and empathetically feel would hurt us and others.

I imitated Dr. Daniel Siegel's model, as seen on YouTube, by illustrating with my fist the three interactive parts of the brain. Siegel explains, "Put your thumb in the middle of your palm and then curl your fingers over the top. You'll have a pretty handy model of the brain. The face of the person is in front of the knuckles, the back of the head toward the back of your hand. Your wrist represents the spinal cord, rising from the backbone, upon which the brain sits. If you lift up your fingers and raise your thumb, you'll see the inner brainstem represented in your palm. Place your thumb back down and you'll see the approximate location of the limbic area (ideally we'd have two thumbs, left and right, to make this a symmetric model). Now curl your fingers back over the top and your cortex is in place." Our ancient *reptilian brain* controls arousal, sleep, wakefulness, fight or flight; it receives visual information to coordinate movement, and control breathing, heartbeat and digestion. Our *limbic system* with its central position in the brain is the core of emotions, deeply rooted in the body, giving richness to conscious experience. The *cerebral cortex,* with its right and left hemispheres, regulates the way we perceive, interpret and adapt to our world. We endeavor to control our negative emotional impulses by focusing on the positive, redirecting our attention and will, even if problematic urges arise, which most likely they will. We create a space within ourselves where we can relax, pause and think before destructive actions are expressed in hurtful ways that we usually regret. Siegel urges children to balance and integrate the instinctual-emotional "downstairs (brain stem and limbic system) and thinking-decision making upstairs (cerebral cortex)" brain.

In *The Whole-Brain Child*, Dr. Siegel emphasizes the need to model behavior and attitude for our students and each other. He relates the story of the discovery of "mirror neurons" in an early 1990s study of a macaque monkey's brain. "They had implanted electrodes to monitor individual neurons, and when the monkey ate a peanut, a certain electrode fired. No surprise there. . . . But then a scientist's snack changed the course of our insight into the mind. One of the researchers picked up a peanut and ate it as the monkey watched. In response, the monkey's motor neuron fired—the same one that had fired when he had actually eaten the peanut himself! The researchers discovered that the monkey's brain was influenced and became active just by *watching* the actions of another. . . . [Mirror neurons] might be the root of empathy. . . . We see an act, we understand the purpose of the act, and we ready ourselves to mirror it." Learning takes place in relational, emotional-social contexts.

Right-brain/left-brain studies help educators understand the different ways students learn, and how to encourage the healthy complementarity of left and right side learning and behavior. Though we are most likely dominant in one hemisphere, learning is optimal when the two halves are working together. In 1981, Robert W. Sperry, along with David Hunter Hubel and Torsten Nils Wiesel, won the Nobel Prize for their "split-brain" study of epileptic patients. In 1940, neurosurgeon William Van Wagenen surgically removed the brain's corpus callosum, composed of 300 million nerve fibers, which connects and facilitates communication between the two sides of the brain. He found the operation could reduce, and even eliminate seizures. In 1974, based on studies of the patients who underwent this surgery, Sperry wrote: "Each hemisphere is indeed a conscious system in its own right, perceiving, thinking remembering, reasoning, willing, and emoting, all at a characteristically human level . . . both the right and left hemispheres may be conscious simultaneously in different, even in mutually conflicting mental experiences." Sperry espoused an asymmetrical model of the brain, whereas other scientists proposed symmetrical models of dynamically connected right and left hemispheres. The left brain, directing the right side of the body, processes speech, sequential thinking (time-conscious), short-term memory, and logic. The right hemisphere, connected to the left side of the body, processes emotion, intuition, sensibilities, retrieval of autobiographical memory, non-verbal communication, and spatial processes. Our left brain deals with one thing at a time, whereas our right brain accommodates several details at the same time. Our right hemisphere is more sensitive to bodily sensations and to our reptilian brain.

We all tend to have a dominant hemisphere, which affects how we learn. Some students may learn through words, others by utilizing maps, or both maps and words. A student may learn a subject through writing/reading, gathering information and synthesizing it into summary ideas. Another learns best through discussion or using visual media, such as interactive websites offered by museums; some "feel it" through art, music, movement and craft. Most students learn in a variety of ways, and respond well to educators who present ideas linearly, visually, and artistically. Gregory Mitchell illustrates the significance of maintaining two intact, interacting hemispheres of the brain with an example: "A person without a right hemisphere could tune a guitar using a pitch pipe; he may be able to play the odd note if it is written down on a piece of paper, and in a very artificial way play some very simple tunes, but this would be done at a robotic level. With the other side of the brain, a person may easily translate intention into action at the non-verbal level. Both types of consciousness are necessary in most activities.... Full consciousness arises from an integration of the two sets of mental processes, which involve a cooperative or collaborative relationship between the two sides of the brain." Mitchell, author of *Man with a Shattered World*, tells the story of a soldier who was wounded and left with a damaged right side of the brain. "When eating soup, when he concentrated on the soup, the spoon disappeared; when he concentrated on the spoon, the soup disappeared; and when he concentrated on the flavor, the whole room disappeared. Restricted only to the left hemisphere, he could linearly attend to one detail at a time."

Educators are starting to pay more attention to the right brain. In his book, *A Whole New Mind: Why Right Brainers Will Rule the Future*, Daniel H. Pink summarizes: "Leading a healthy, happy successful life depends on 'both' hemispheres of your brain. But the contrast in how our cerebral hemispheres operate does yield a powerful *metaphor* for how individuals and organizations navigate their lives. Some people seem more comfortable with logical, sequential, computer-like reasoning. They tend to become lawyers, accountants, and engineers. Other people are more comfortable with holistic, intuitive, and nonlinear reasoning. They tend to become inventors, entertainers, and counselors.... L-Directed [left-brain] aptitudes—the sort of things measured by the SAT and deployed by CPAs—are still necessary. But they're no longer sufficient. Instead, the R-Directed [right-brain] aptitudes so often disdained and dismissed—artistry, empathy, taking the long view, pursuing the transcendent—will increasingly determine who soars and who stumbles."

We need not exaggerate or absolutize some of the studies about the two hemispheres. Teens gifted in math are found to be strong in both hemispheres: "It's not that you have a special math module somewhere in your brain, but rather that the brain's particular functional organization ... predisposes it toward the use of high level imagery and spatial skills which in turn just happens to be very useful when it comes to doing math reasoning" (Michael W. O'Boyle, PhD, University of Melbourne).

Over the years, my students have taken "Right-Brain, Left-Brain" tests to discover if they were double-dominant, or right or left dominant. Such tests determine where one's inclinations, strengths and weaknesses are, and how to fine-tune the collective work of the two hemispheres. After viewing Steven Spielberg's *Lincoln*, an outgoing, long-black-haired sophomore, Leonora, who is involved in activism for women's and children's rights, commented: "We're studying Lincoln in history, and I've been learning about the effects of black slavery on the United States. Spielberg's movie allowed me to vicariously feel Lincoln, to understand Lincoln's human touch, his humorous stories, and craftiness to get what he wanted, an amendment abolishing slavery. I am interested in the works of organizations dedicated to end modern human slavery. The movie inspired me."

Recently I took a "Hemispheric Dominance Inventory" test on a Middle Tennessee State University website. Asked nineteen questions, I answered seven as "left brain," and twelve as "right brain." I use the cognitive processes of my right brain the most, tending to be holistic rather than detail oriented; preferring concrete, kinesthetic learning; intuitively checking whether something "feels right," rather than only being logical. When I'm overly logical or excessively emotional, out of balance, I tend to make poor decisions. Such tests provide guidelines and demonstrate varying degrees of inclinations, learning styles, and the coordination and synchronism of the two hemispheres of the cortex. Studies of people who have lost right-brain functioning show such individuals still have some creative ability. Analyzing and imagining stimulate both sides of the brain. As Kendra Cherry, author and educator, says, "Right/left brain studies have a basis in fact that has been dramatically distorted and exaggerated." Though these studies are relatively recent, they have been helpful to students who want clarity about how the right brain processes emotion and body language (sensory awareness) and how the left brain processes words, sentences, logic, organization, breaking it down step by step (rational awareness). Buoyed by the conviction that they can have some control over their thoughts and emotions, and can heal their brains, students strive for rational and emotional resilience. Realizing the importance of slowing down and releasing stress, they engage right-brain experiences which give them sensorial feelings in the here and now.

An enthusiastic sophomore, beginning the process of sorting out requests for dates, explained how she was more sensitive to "the gut, the belly" as a way of knowing how she might respond. Eminent scholar Michael Saso, citing *The Second Brain* by Michael D. Gershon, MD, recently talked about scientific studies suggesting a "second brain," the enteric brain, the web of neurons throughout the gastrointestinal tract. These studies validate the importance of being centered in the belly and gut instinct, "common sense" to many. Tending to dwell too much in my head, I find it illuminating that some students talk about "head and heart," how they learn in different, sometimes conflicting ways. "My head tells me no. My heart tells me yes, my head yes, my heart no." Interviewing Philip Shepherd, author of *New Self, New World: Recovering Our Senses in the Twenty-First Century*, Amnon Buchbinder starts the conversation: "If cranial thinking sets us apart from the world, the thinking in the belly joins us to it. If the cranial brain believes itself surrounded by a knowable world that can be controlled, the brain in our belly is in touch with the world's mystery . . . this suggests how complicated our relationship with our bodily intelligence is. . . . Leaving the 'tyrant's castle' of our heads and entering into a profoundly embodied relationship with the mystery and beauty of the world we will successfully turn our planetary crisis into an 'initiation.'"

We can overemphasize activity in our lives and in education. Nancy Pine, author of *Educating Young Giants: What Kids Learn*, was a graduate student in China in 1990. Fascinated by the subject of education, she started a twenty-year study about student strengths and weaknesses in the United States and China (better math, more respectful, reluctant to ask questions and express creativity, more parent-directed). Pine cautions, "Generalizations do not apply to all children in a given culture, and we also know they can lead to stereotypes." Pine welcomed Feng, her long-time research colleague from China visiting the United States, for an outing at the zoo. Over the years, they compared different learning patterns in the two countries. After visiting the zoo, Feng lamented: "The parents weren't talking to their children about the animals. How can they learn anything if they don't point things out to them?" Pine laughed good-heartedly: "It was Saturday, and they were here to relax, to enjoy the animals on a family outing. Children don't need to be instructed all the time."

Being sensitive to the innate talents and affinities of our children, we can nourish and support them, whatever their level. With loving patience, wise use of technical & scientific knowledge and aesthetic & kinesthetic sensitivity, parents and educators are planting seeds of knowledge in their children, and they in us. Children and adolescents require care and attention; there's no magic pill to accelerate the growth of our students. However, educators are not ignoring the implications of modern neuroscientific brain studies. Instructors want to understand the emotional aspects of teaching, tuning into the emotions and body language of the students, as well as assessing and aiming presentations tailored to each student's unique learning capacity.

A discouraged high-school senior who managed B's with the help of classmates, told me of her struggle to get through pages of material that were too difficult for her to comprehend: "I wish I could learn at a slower pace. I end up copying and memorizing my friends' homework. I just have to get a good SAT score, but when can I study for it? You recommend that the students study at least one to two hours, three evenings a week, practicing sections of the test in the month before the actual test. We can check our answers in the back of the SAT book and understand the explanations of the answers. Grading each section, we know where we stand. We also plan to practice three full-length tests in the month. Yet I've only studied two evenings in the last three weeks and taken one practice test with a terrible result. I'm not ready; I want to study this week, but the teachers give us a lot of homework." Some teachers, perhaps too few, work with the student, so he or she can hand in assignments at a later date in order to prepare for the SAT exam. Now through online learning, students can finish courses at their own pace. Sometimes they need to concentrate on preparing for tests required for college applicants.

As much as I want students to work diligently, I'm convinced that a balanced approach is the most functional and healthy. Some teachers are giving too much homework. I understand the need to do extra study for tests, but homework should be creatively prepared and corrected, reasonably assigned in coordination with all the teachers and SAT examination dates. Some teachers are flexible about assignment due dates. My students remind me that they do not all learn at the same pace.

Through the Internet, via smartphones, the global brain is continually connecting, disconnecting, and strengthening, like a teen growing into pre-frontal cortex maturity. Such promise is an opportunity, but not a guarantee of success. Through electrochemical messaging, the brain mysteriously produces mind, at best a neural symphony or at worst a cacophonous orchestra. Usually we live between the extremes of highs and lows, which come and go. Teens are learning skills to react sensibly to both. Luckily for most of us, our lives are happy, not besieged too often, but disasters do happen prompting the need to prepare our children.

Scientific findings demonstrate that the teenage mind has an exceptional ability to successfully encode cognitive and emotional knowledge needed for survival and prosperity in our global society. Teens struggle between reactive, emotional impulses and more reasoned, thoughtful motivations. They are coordinating the right and left sides of their brains, their heads and hearts, cranial and enteric brains. Emotion, thinking, and habit determine the quality of our lives. Through life and educational experiences, our students become co-creators of an unpredictable but fascinating future. We are humbled by our inadequate theories. Albert Schweitzer says it well. "As soon as man does not take his existence for granted, but beholds it as something unfathomably mysterious, thought begins."

****

Encode

*A linguistics professor was lecturing to his
class one day. In English, he said, a double
negative forms a positive. In some languages,
though, such as Russian, a double negative is
still a negative. However, there is no language
wherein a double positive can form a negative.
A voice from the back of the room piped up,
"Yeah, right."*
—Ballast Quarterly Review

*Get it down. Take a chance. It may be bad, but
it's the only way you can do anything good.*
—William Faulkner

Students often resist the effort necessary to improve writing skills for the twenty-five minute SAT essay. I know it's difficult for most of us to write, as Sidney Sheldon aptly says: "A blank piece of paper is God's way of telling us how hard it is to be God." The students need writing practice and must be reminded and encouraged through good instruction and teaching materials to master the basics of writing. I use "speed writing" to help them think more quickly, and learn to perform within time limits. "Just write." One student liked to say, "Fake it 'til you make it." The motor skill of writing connects with one's ability to remember, so I encourage students not only to write in the SAT seminar, but also to take notes in class, which improves listening skills. The students read aloud in order for the material to be processed actively in the auditory channel of the brain. ("I know it but I can't say it. . . . I understand it, but I can't put it in writing.") The class has the opportunity to listen and give opinions. ("Just doesn't sound smooth. . . . Liked that. . . . What about . . . ?") We spend time playing with the words to create a more cogent and flowing essay. Some students decline to have their essays read aloud, but seem to enjoy listening and commenting. Corrections and suggestions are incorporated into the final paper.

I want to be sure the students are satisfied with explanations and can express concepts verbally and in writing. It's tough to get students to proofread and re-write papers. Teachers implore them to appreciate that it is the process of editing and revising that embodies the art and craft of writing. Elmore Leonard mused, "If it sounds like writing, I rewrite it." I ask the students to do revisions, but there's often a reluctance "to do it again." In an interview, Ernest Hemingway said, "I rewrote the ending of *Farewell to Arms*, the last page of it, thirty-nine times before I was satisfied." Ask what stumped him, he replied, "Getting the words right." Noel Coward once commented on Edna Ferber's tailored suit, "Edna, you look almost like a man." Ferber, getting her words just right, replied: "So do you."

Writing with impact is a work of science and art, which is accomplished only through the revision process. Even if the student does not become an adept writer, basic writing mechanics and an appreciation of the aesthetic arrangement of words are emphasized. Transferring one's thoughts into the written word takes time and effort. The discipline of writing is difficult for most of us. After correcting errors, praising positive qualities, and offering suggestions, I ask the students to rewrite, encouraging them to get past their reluctance to give the mental exertion required. Writing can be creative, an art form as well as a technique. "Get words onto the paper; later, your work will be an art form which gives a sense of satisfaction. It's our nature to be creative." Another writing problem pupils encounter is getting started. We practice outlining and free-writing without worrying about grammar. Even though a student had difficulty writing a practice SAT essay, the aspiring writer told me he preferred to spend the time working on a novel: "It's a waste of time writing such short pieces." Soon he realized he had to start more humbly, from the simple to the complex, by first writing short pieces well. Learning builds on mastering stepping stones to the knowledge/skill desired.

Admirer: Herr Mozart, I'm thinking of writing symphonies. Can you give me any suggestions on how to get started?

Mozart: A symphony is a very complex musical form. Perhaps you should begin with some simple *lieder* and work your way up to a symphony.

Admirer: But Herr Mozart, you were writing symphonies when you were eight years old.

Mozart: But I never asked anybody how.

A cheerful yet hyperactive student would only write for five or ten minutes when practicing a twenty-five minute SAT essay. In addition to five-minute speed writing exercises, I asked him to practice the SAT essay for eight to ten minutes with full attention, increasing the time periods until he was ready to practice twenty-five minutes. I encouraged him to ask for suggestions.

****

Bamboo Bending

*Moody. Impulsive. Maddening. Why do
teenagers act the way they do? Viewed through
the eyes of evolution, their most exasperating
traits may be the key to success as adults.*
—National Geographic, *Oct. 2011*

*At bottom, each person is asking, "Who am I
really? How can I get in touch with this real
self, underlying all my surface behavior? How
can I become myself?"*
—Carl Rogers

I am more patient and adaptable to the individual
student than when I began teaching; I'm not as
frustrated when my expectations, although still high,
are not met. One student had no energy for class; he
was listless and "in his own world." I encouraged him
to no avail. Later I learned his parents were going
through a nasty divorce. Our children live in a
stressful world. On December 16, 2012, the *Los Angeles
Times* referred to the Newtown, Connecticut school
massacre, with the poignant headline "Heroism,
Helplessness." On the front page were heartbreaking
photos of six-year olds, lovely Emilie Parker and
innocent Noah Panzer, two of Sandy Hook Elementary
School's twenty-six murder victims. The world wept at
this sacrilegious, horrific act and reached out to the
Connecticut community. High-school and adult
students practice fire and earthquake drills, simulate
protective actions, such as lock-downs, hiding, and
navigating escape routes to use in case of an attack.
Some virtual, interactive game programs train students
in safety under varying circumstances. I remember
ducking into underground fallout shelters in the
1950s, shielding myself in case of an actual nuclear
attack with its radioactive debris. Though our schools
are continually improving security, terrifying random

attacks have been emotionally encoded into the consciousness of our students and community.

Educators apply discoveries from social neuroscience in developing effective strategies to teach content and meta-skills. I was captivated by an article in the October 2011 *National Geographic*, "Beautiful Brains," by David Dobbs. The cover is an artistic tribute to the exquisite complexity and impressionability of the teenager: a white silhouette of a teen head with orange, yellow, purple, blue, and green globes floating from the top of the cranium, out and up into a black space of infinite possibilities. The caption, "we're not as crazy as you think" foreshadows an understanding of the intricate adaptability and basic soundness of the teen brain. To support and teach the teenager the best ways possible, educators are studying the way the brain-mind, conscious and unconscious, works. Educators are sneaky. They urge students to study the subjects, not just to learn the body of knowledge, but more so to train and fine-tune the students' mental capacities. Neuroscientists, through imaging, show us the activity within the brain that produces thoughts, emotions, and intentions. We're learning how the brain works, and that we can influence and synchronize the quality of our mind and emotions.

We—parents, students, business people, and entrepreneurs—are pulling together, even in a time when we feel bent because of the severe economic downturn in the global economy. Informed by remarkable technological, neuropsychological, and educational advances for our students, educators address the student as physical, intellectual, emotional and spiritual beings. We can change our brains, our emotions, and our relationships; but to be effective, we have to do it naturally and intelligently. Like every species, human beings evolve. We use our minds to invent a flying machine, discover powerful medicines, and program computers with massive amounts of information, which we put at our fingertips through smartphones. Today we may feel stressed like bamboo reeds in a fierce tropical storm, but we are not broken. Moving forward as a society, we have profited from science; we benefit from technology, neuroscience, and scholarly, innovative educational theory to improve the quality of our children's education. We must pass on humanistic, moral, and wise counsel to our students.

Teachers observe their students grow emotionally, clumsily at first, but slowly adapting, understanding, dealing with stress, and collaborating to meet new challenges. Our society needs many professionals, technicians, and service-oriented workers; it is often in high school that a student must start to consider his future role in society. The students are exposed to subjects they might resist, for some it's math and science, for others languages and humanities. "Why do I have to take physics and chemistry? I'm never going to be a scientist." The teacher responds: "Your responsibility is to take the basic courses to know what a scientist is and does. Then you have some experience from which you can decide." Some high-school students are late-bloomers who need time to comprehend subjects they may have initially pushed away. Einstein's teachers thought he was unable to grasp mathematics. Can you imagine thinking Einstein was slow in math? It takes time to finds one's educational niche. Think about baseball in America with its demanding process of choosing top players. Starting from Little League, there's a selection process. Everyone stops playing after a while. Maybe 90% of the kids are playing tee ball; then 80% play machine pitch, 30% in middle school, 10% in high school, 5% in college, and .001 % in the big leagues. It is a weeding out process just like education. Like Tiger Moms, parents and teachers often compel students to persevere through resisted basic subjects. Students need a fundamental understanding from which to make important decisions about their future study and work.

****

We use our left hemisphere's linguistic packets to ask another person's left hemisphere a question about his experiences or feelings (or ask ourselves the same question). That person must decode those signals and send a message across the corpus callosum to activate the right hemisphere, which comes up with the nonverbal somatic-sensory images that are the "stuff" of feelings. He then has to reverse the process translating the right hemisphere's internal music back into the digital neural-processors of the left hemisphere's language centers. Then a sentence is spoken. Amazing.
—Daniel Siegel

Scientists explain that adolescent brains, from age twelve to twenty-five, become more sophisticated, capable, and speedy. The brain expands networks and connections, just like the Internet. The intricate inter-wiring of the brain becomes solid as nerve fibers (axons) are securely insulated. Neurons utilize long nerve fibers to send signals, which are retrieved by branchlike extensions (dendrites). Sending and receiving communication, direction, and coordination are all orchestrated like a symphony of lights in the brain. At the same time, the brain's chemical passageways (synapses) through which axons and dendrites pass, transform, becoming stronger, and more functional. The brain cortex discards unused synapses. Center of much of our conscious thinking, the brain cortex becomes thinner but more pliable;

the frontal brain is capable of nuanced thinking and boundless imagination. Though a teenager is physiologically receptive for new wiring and learning, patience is required during bumpy times of growth. "When this development proceeds normally, we get better at balancing impulse, desire, goals, self-interest, rules, ethics, and even altruism, generating behavior that is more complex and sometimes at least, more sensible. But at times, and especially at first, the brain does this work clumsily. It's hard to get all those new cogs to mesh" (*National Geographic*).

> *The ancient 'reptilian' brain is fast, bossy, sure of itself and never shuts up. The modern brain, primarily in the cortex, is reflective, slow, conflicted and often defers to its elder. In the time it takes the reflective brain to give you a long-winded lecture on the perils of sweet greasy food, the reptile has you on your second jelly doughnut.*
> —K. C. Cole

Choosing the topic "Habit in My Life" the students wrote about the necessity for automatic habits to negotiate ordinary living. They also described good and bad habits related to one's study and character. A high-school junior felt he was becoming a better student as he overcame his habitual resistance by "just starting, forcing myself as I might start a cross country run. My long-term awareness has helped me diminish my need for instant gratification. I have a goal to win by scoring the best grades possible." One student linked the level of her attention to sufficient sleep and food. During deep sleep, short-term memories in the hippocampus transfer to long-term memory in the prefrontal cortex, one activity among the many going on. Diet is likewise important. Feeling hungry takes away the energy needed to exert self-control and distinguish long and short-term awareness. Once I was driving in my old neighborhood of many years and had a sudden automatic tendency to turn right to my old apartment. I flinched to the right in response to my ingrained program suited to a past time, but I didn't turn. I was witnessing an embodied habitual response weaken. What we don't activate eventually becomes obsolete. Certainly the students have more significant habits to overcome.

Studies of adolescents show an imbalance between the development of the subcortical limbic system (emotional) and the prefrontal cortical region (controlling). Teens are more susceptible to anxiety if they fail to handle stress. They suffer a relatively high rate of affective disorders, suicides and accidental deaths (*Developmental Psychobiology*, In Press, Sackler Institute, Weil Cornell Medical College, NY). According to the Centers for Disease Control and Prevention, 8% of adolescents suffer mental problems, such as attention-deficit hyperactivity, oppositional defiance, depression, and anxiety. Rapid and uneven development has consequences in the law. Missouri's highest court, with the advice of eight medical and mental health organizations, spared a seventeen-year-old from the death penalty. "Adolescents are immature in the very fibers of their brains, so seventeen-year-olds shouldn't have full criminal responsibility for capital crimes" (PBS, October 13, 2004). While developing, teens may feel awkward physically, intellectually, and socially; yet teens are quick to learn, if their attention is piqued. Intelligence (IQ) and emotional intelligence (EQ) can improve. Cathy Price, University College London, writes: "We have a tendency to assess children and determine the course of their education relatively early in life. But we have been shown that their intelligence is likely to be still developing. We have to be careful not to write off poorer performers at an early age when in fact their IQ may improve significantly given a few more years."

Baldwin Park Adult School conducted classes at a large hospital facility for severely challenged students. I worked with a team of dedicated, caring teachers and staff who discovered that these students benefited from a basic education. Psychologists taught us that nonverbal intelligence could be nourished and assessed just as verbal intelligence. Several students could not speak or were limited in speech. Psychologists were able to bypass language barriers in evaluating overall intellectual ability, at whatever level. Knowing the students could progress, the teachers would model steps of a task through "hands on" guiding, for example steadying and directing a student's hand to paint different colors on a large white drawing pad or solve number puzzles. We organized community outings, which served social intelligence and practical living skills; sometimes we participated in stimulating experiences (at a mall, picnic or video arcade) and other times more calming recreation, at a small petting zoo or in the park on a beautiful day. Non-verbal students had unique and meaningful ways to communicate, as the teachers often witnessed. With some one-on-one attention, we utilized pictures, films, and slide-shows. Some students had electronic speech-generating communication boards with pictures, numbers, the alphabet, basic commands and answers, symbols, gestures and signs. One teacher told me: "This is a tough job but at the same time a lot of fun; I find it rewarding being closely involved, even in a small way, with Special Education students." The teachers usually enjoyed going to work, despite disruptions and emergencies, which often occurred amidst this fragile population.

****

Encode

Researchers have actually found that they (teens) don't think they're invincible. They know they can die. And they also don't underestimate risk. What they do is they overestimate risk less than adults do. If you screen them to see if they understand risk, they understand [it] actually better than adults do. They just don't exaggerate the risk as much. And the big difference, there are rewards in some situations—like driving fast down the highway with your friends—that they care more about than adults will, which is why it's not that they don't understand the risk. It's that the balance changes. They see more benefit in certain things.
—David Dobbs

Announcing that he and a few others were getting knives to confront an adversarial group to settle an inter-ethnic argument, a skinny sixteen-year-old boy came rushing into class. His excited sense of inflated power was met by other students' advice that he should avoid the risky confrontation. He wanted to show he was tough, but was obviously relieved when his peers advised against such action. It was clear how much acceptance by peers meant to him. Sometimes during a break, students stay in the classroom and speak with each other as if I weren't there, yet perhaps wanting me on some level to be a sounding board. I have peripherally heard some of my students speak about sex, drugs, food, parents, siblings, teachers, homework, colleges, careers, dating, video games, boyfriend-girlfriend, music, movies, culture, and gay rights.

As a teenager, I did some foolish things to be accepted and welcomed by my peers. Teenagers sometimes seem intrigued by risk and danger. Out of character, as if I didn't have a will of my own, I engaged in impulsive and perilous car-racing activities during my senior year of high school. Feeling brave, in a challenge, I would pull up to another car. We'd floor our vehicles for a daring sprint. I'd cheer on other racers who likewise enjoyed the underground drama (unimagined by parents) of late night racing. We would find isolated streets to compete; a cheering audience would disappear before police arrived. Heart beating wildly, I was both excited and afraid. Perhaps some of today's youth in Saudi Arabia, who take part in a form of street racing and stunt driving called "drifting," have that same feeling of stretching conventional restrictions and defying mortality. In truth, it was excessive self-indulgence, wanting thrills at a disproportionate cost/risk to others and myself. When my friend crashed his car—luckily he was uninjured— seeing the bent steel and jagged glass, I lost my taste for racing. My resolve was strong enough to resist invitations to again join the street-racing scene.

A former student, Jimmy Hua, introduced me to the sport of parkour. A participant, a traceur, navigates a route, typically in a city, trying to get around or through various obstacles in the quickest and most efficient manner possible: jumping, climbing, or running. Jimmy said parkour, with its liberating free motion enabled him to manage basic fears of risk-taking. Psychologist Laurence Steinberg from Temple University proposes that over the course of human evolution, the willingness to take risks during this period of life has given humans an adaptive edge. Teens are both physically magnificent and emotionally vulnerable. Citing the parkour slogan— *Live life; nothing starts until you take action*—Jimmy related the following account. "I begin my run, and I think of all the possible ways I might fail and injure myself. There's always that possibility, since parkour is hard. Only a few are able to parkour. I get really nervous, but once the camera starts rolling and my friends say 'Action!' I forget all my fears in a flash. I take off at full speed, inching closer and closer to my first obstacle, a round table. I think, 'How can I get over the table? Should I do a monkey vault, kong vault, speed vault, or dash vault?' I make my decision quickly. I dash vault over the table with ease, maintaining my momentum. Keep going; don't stop; be aware of your surroundings, stay alert, confident. It's instinctual now; I'm in the flow. My next obstacle is an up-coming bench without a backrest. I think about doing a front-flip off the bench and then a barrel roll. I run out of time for second thoughts. I take off with one foot and land on the bench. Punching off the bench, I swing my arms forward and tuck my legs. I'm spinning and as I land on the balls of my feet, the momentum forces me slightly forward, giving me the impetus for my barrel roll. I push from the ground as a finish to my roll and take off without losing speed. A wall twice my height is up next. There's only one thing for me to do, plant one foot on the wall and kick myself up. I thought how easy this was, since it was only a kick-up off a wall. Plant and kick, grab and haul myself up onto the roof of a building. I think about how high I am, and that I can't do this. The next moment my fear of heights disappears, and I'm flying off the building, and the next thing I know, I'm on the ground again, doing a barrel roll.

"'Cut! Awesome!' my friend yells out. He asks me if I was scared. I said I was, but the adrenaline buried the fears. Doing parkour is exciting and fun. I act outside my comfort zone. Two days later, the parkour video is on YouTube. I have engraved on my heart and soul that success never comes without failures. Never let laughs intimidate you for what you do imperfectly. You'll be better and stronger in the future."

****

Bamboo Bending

As we move through adolescence, the brain undergoes extensive remodeling, resembling a network and wiring upgrade. . . . The adaptive-adolescent story casts the teen less as a rough draft than as an exquisitely sensitive, highly adaptable creature wired almost perfectly for the job of moving from the safety of home into the complicated world outside.
—1990s National Institute of Health Teen Study

As teenagers, we are figuring out how we will survive in the greater society, moving from dependence to independence; to make that happen, we pursue a network of friends and resources beyond family. Teenagers are excited to explore new worlds, yet unprepared to give up the security of the child's safe haven of home. The teenager experiences a predicament: he is feeling impulsive, and adventuresome, but at the same time confronted by society's demand for self-control. Teens crave more independence but are dependent on their families. Parents and teachers have a responsibility to aid the teenager in making this transition to adult independence. The most important motivation to become a good person and student starts from within. Enthusiasm for learning makes all the difference in the world, but doesn't come easily for some. "Sorry, Mr. Morgan, I can't get my brain to work today. I'm so tired." As coach, the teacher knows when to urge the student to study and when to take a break. Resting is part of learning, a time when the fruits of study percolate and integrate below the conscious level. Sleep and relaxation are essential. One student managed well by only sleeping six hours a night, but required the freedom to sleep in on the weekend, which recharged and refreshed him. His parents were supportive. The promise of sleeping in on weekends gave him the strength during the week to study late. A University of Washington study of fruit flies demonstrates how sleep influences memory consolidation, the ability of important memories to be stored and made accessible (*Science* magazine, June 2011). The fruit flies were trained to perform a task and then given four hours of induced sleep. They were able to complete the task well, but similarly trained fruit flies without sleep were not.

Some administrations are in favor of a school day that starts and ends later. High schools will continue to offer more flexible scheduling, with online and DVD courses and intense seminars, as well as attendance at the high-school campus for teacher-instruction, discussion, socializing, and learning collaboratively. Barbara Strauch, a deputy science editor of the *New York Times*, succinctly makes the case for starting school later (or having that option): "If teenagers sleep until noon in part because shifts in brain chemicals make them drowsy later—and because they're deeply sleep-deprived from getting up at dawn to get to high schools that begin ridiculously early—why can't schools start later?" Strauch, in *The Primal Teen*, goes on to ask educators and parents to be balanced in the amount of homework and extra-curricular activities they ask from students. "After reviewing findings from adolescent sleep research, even the US Navy decided last year to let new recruits—most of them still teenagers themselves—stay up later, sleep later, and get eight hours of sleep instead of six, a model that used to be standard but had been forgotten. If the military can do this, why can't the rest of us?"

****

Bamboo Bending

Teachers must have the greatest respect for the young personality, realizing that in the soul of the adolescent, great values are hidden, and that in the minds of these boys and girls, there lies all our hope of future progress and the judgment of our times.
—Dr. Maria Montessori

A few years ago, a girl asked me to review her paper about the theme of alienation in the book, *The Catcher in the Rye.* Sympathetic to Holden Caulfield, who considered the adult world phony, she told me: "Sometimes I face the cynical, hypocritical side of the adult society, which pretends to welcome us, but is dog-eat-dog. At times I find myself angry and judgmental, standing outside society. Is the adult world one I really want to join? Is it a happy world? I'm faced with withdrawing into my own world like Holden did *or* joining the human race. I can isolate myself or make some real friends, connecting with society." This conversation brought me back to my high-school reading of *The Catcher in the Rye* and how it awakened me to adult hypocrisy. I thought I could evaluate my parents and the world with simple answers. I felt a "sense of superiority" and distrust, luckily short-lived. Perhaps such rebellion is a natural phase of a young person's evolution, preparing adolescents to take over for adults. Teenagers not only find themselves conflicted, but also enjoy the ebullience of new growth, friends, abilities, and self-confidence. For most of my students—full of life—it is an amazing experience of growth. In 2012, eternally glowing, youthful man-teen Dick Clark died. He is identified with the highlighted flavors of adolescence: freshness, love of cars, music, movies, dance, electronics, fashion, first dates, making out, romantic sensibilities, getting crushes, getting crushed, heightened sexual capacity, fuller bodies, changing voices, cliques, being "in" and "out," parents, siblings and peers. With the exception of infancy, teens are growing faster than at any other stage of development. By the age of six, the brain has 95% of an adult-sized brain; during adolescence the cerebrum continues to grow its ability to think, reason, and formulate abstract ideas. I am fortunate: a co-teacher with my students, co-learners on this wild, unpredictable journey through life.

3

Adapt

We are quite naturally impatient in everything to reach the end without delay. We should like to skip the intermediate stages. We are impatient of being on the way to something unknown, something new. And yet it is the law of all progress that it is made by passing through some stages of instability— and that it may take a very long time. And so I think it is with you, your ideas mature gradually—let them grow; let them shape themselves, without undue haste. Don't try to force them on, as though you could be today what time (that is to say, grace and circumstances acting on your own good will) will make of you tomorrow.
—Pierre Teilhard de Chardin

Fareed Zakaria wrote about the decline of US education and what we should do about it (*Time* magazine, November 14, 2011). Zakaria praises the remarkable technologist and entrepreneur Steve Jobs and his first-rate public high school (Homestead High, Cupertino California). High school prepared Jobs for outstanding achievement. Today the United States high-school education system is ranked 26th in the world (World Economic Forum). Like the United States, California, my home state, is "at the bottom of the industrialized world by most measures of educational achievement"; 69% of US 8th graders are below proficient in reading, 68% in math (National Center for Education Statistics: "Special Analysis 2010"). Upper mobility requires education, whether in high school, college, trade school or advanced mentoring. Even those with college degrees, perhaps in disciplines not carefully chosen, face uncertain employment prospects. "While we have been sleeping, the rest of the world has been upgrading its skills. . . . Other countries have focused on math and science, while in America, degrees have proliferated in 'fields' like sports exercise and leisure studies." Zakaria's solution: *work harder and longer; hire the best teachers; and be flexible.* Zakaria acknowledges that most teacher unions are against longer hours, but presently many US schools do not meet the needs of students who are transitioning rapidly into new times. There are one thousand schools in thirty-eight states that have longer days. Some math teachers praise the opportunity to have ninety-minute classes instead of the ordinary fifty-minute class. Even if the school day is not lengthened, there are contemporary schools that experiment with some longer classes along with fifty-minute classes.

Our school system is lagging behind the world, but fortunately seems to be slowly waking up. Educators seek to create a technologically advanced, socially healthy environment with excellent high-school teachers using state-of-the-art methods, materials, and media. Bill Gates says, "So the basic research into great teaching, that's now become our biggest investment." In Finland, demanding and creative training programs for teachers only accept one in ten applicants; in the United States, the teaching profession is not held in such high esteem. "Finnish students score near the very top on international tests, yet they do not follow the Asian model of study, study and more study. Instead they start school a year later than most, emphasize creative work and shun tests for most of the year." One can't argue with Finland's success, but here in the United States, at our particular stage of growth as educators, we need to appreciate both the Finnish success and the Asian model of intense study, adapting psychological and educational insights related to US high-school life. Students today aspire to have a stronger say in how they pursue their education in cooperation with the teacher, and desire a hands-on, tech-savvy approach.

****

> *There is no more dreadful punishment than*
> *futile and hopeless labor.*
> —Albert Camus

We are all aware of what's at stake in preparing for a rapidly advancing global economy. The challenge is for our children to master the skills necessary to adapt wherever in the world they may be needed while remaining true to themselves, to their own longings and unique abilities. "I don't want to be educated for the past, but for the future," a student reminded me. Our times are a metaphor for adolescent growth: rapid change, chaos, intriguing possibilities, challenges of less dependence, unknowns, risks, and vulnerabilities in the face of Mother Nature and armed terrorists. An article in the *Huffington Post* by Robert Reich states that Apple Computer employs only 43,000 Americans in the United States, but over 700,000 workers in China can be mobilized at any hour to make Apple products. Reich says not to fault Apple; they're paid to make the best in the cheapest way and cannot be blamed. "Problem is, a large and growing portion of our workforce isn't equipped to be productive. Put simply, American workers are hobbled by deteriorating schools, unaffordable college tuitions, decaying infrastructure."

Zakaria encourages teachers to involve students to be attentive and active in learning. Students want teachers with a sense of humor but who keep the class focused, work hard, prepare, correct assignments, give individual attention, and keep learning to teach the most up-to-date knowledge effectively. The student can clarify and reinforce the lesson via the Internet, textbook, and notes from the "boring" lecture. There's a growing trend for educators to teach collaboratively, making use of individual skills, which when implemented as a whole, make for a dynamic school. Being part of a team, teachers who are not adept lecturers can instead concentrate on "hands on" learning, Internet-supported presentations, DVDs of movies and expert lecturers, and other electronic and interactive expositions of educational materials.

According to the Pew Research Center's Internet and American Life Project, 40% of teachers/students use tablets, in some cases replacing textbooks. A teacher commented about his digitally-grown students. "It's great that a student can use a tablet to supplement the textbook or perhaps replace it. I can use features such as language translators, videos, contemporary events, virtual experiments, and tests with cogent explanations of the answers. Teachers want technical training. I've wasted time in class trying to use my smart board before being knowledgeable about it. Though not a panacea, technology is an important tool among several which can serve the students and teachers." Just as students have unique learning styles, teachers have special teaching abilities, weaknesses, and strengths. Successful educational administrators build on individual teacher strength, and don't insist that educators instruct in one particular way. Schools in our liberal society have a variety of teachers who walk slightly different paths toward academics, but share the common goal of wanting to educate our children.

****

Adapt

The document, "Decision to Deepen Education Reform," reflects the deep concern of China's leaders over the negative consequences of traditional test-oriented education. Its policy goals are straightforward: to emphasize sowing students' creativity and practical abilities over instilling an ability to achieve certain test scores and recite rote knowledge.
—Yong Zhao
(Michigan State University)

China's educational reform is just beginning. 1996 Peace Corps volunteer Peter Hessler recently returned to Fuling, on the Yangtze River, to visit his former students (*National Geographic*, March 2013). He met with Liao Chaoli, English name Mo Money, now a teacher, and Yang Fanglin, Emily, who remembered the time when the government assigned jobs to college graduates. "You didn't have to make many decisions. Now there are so many options, which create pressure." Dai Xiaohong whose English name is William Jefferson Foster in honor of Bill Clinton, tutors English to children of entrepreneurs. Chen Zhenyong is also a teacher and owner of four apartments. Angela Chen adds: "As more and more courses are offered free to anyone with an Internet connection, some American professors have developed a huge following abroad, particularly in China" (*The Chronicle of Higher Education*, March/April 2013). Education is becoming globally available; it's up to adults to create peaceful and learning-conducive conditions, no matter the economic class.

In 2004, Salman Khan boosted the democratization of education by opening Khan Academy, a one-world Internet schoolhouse. The Internet is connecting worldwide, even to classrooms with hard dirt floors. Nine million students take courses every month. The site includes diagnostics, so students can determine what they know and don't know. In the future, such courses will likely be accepted for credit in late high school and community colleges, especially college remedial courses. Such endeavors are not meant to replace teachers and lectures but to complement them and to help individualize instruction and update teaching methods. Face-to-face interaction with teachers and other students plays a vital role in education. Students master subjects at different paces, and can benefit from personalized online instruction, including interactive help requests and responses. Khan cautions that there's no silver bullet, no easy way, but academies such as his are "helping people learn better, giving them tools to take agency of their own learning, thinking behind the formulas, preparing for the outside world, and creating new mind-sets for both student and teacher." Many courses are better presented via media, with teachers helping individual students or problem-solving in small groups. Group reading and writing is helpful not only for learning but for growing social intelligence.

Fareed Zakaria's remarks about his own Asian educational system are significant, but perhaps no longer apply as strictly to today's average student in Asia. Parents and students tell me some schools in China continue to overemphasize rote learning; it takes time to change, despite the directives coming from bureaucrats and education gurus. Fareed Zakaria reflects on studying in India: "It gave me an impressive base of knowledge and taught me how to study hard and fast. But when I got to the United States for college, I found that it had not trained me that well to think. American education at its best teaches you how to solve problems, truly understand the material, question authority, think for yourself and be creative. It teaches you to learn what you love and to love learning. We will succeed not by becoming more Asian." I would add to Zakaria's prescription that the United States revitalize its educational system by building upon its distinctly American character. My experience is that the melding of cultures is nuanced and, despite strong stereotypes, East and West can beneficially complement each other. Our consideration, with and for our children, is a chance to discern together what works, and to devise our own best plan of action to improve and make the most of the high-school experience and our fleeting lives.

Today's students want hands-on opportunities to connect with the community and work beyond high school. Students appreciate the opportunity to work in small ways with business people and professionals, to be mentored in business, engineering, the arts, and vocational skills. A former university classmate, William Muller, is president of Verbum Dei High School in Watts. The high school prepares the student for college and a career. Its corporate work-study internship program gives students on-the-job training, working at law firms, banks, engineering companies, and non-profit entities. Students work five days a month to defray the costs of their $15,000 yearly tuition. Presently no more than $2,700 per year is asked for tuition; the average family pays $1,500. Each corporation or non-profit provides $28,000 (a donated student internship for five students). Students gain valuable experience at high school and in the workplace.

****

I have never let my schooling interfere with my education.
—Mark Twain

When I attended high school, there were few opportunities to be mentored and to volunteer. Today's high school students inspire me with their sense of volunteerism coupled with an interest in acquiring skills that will carry over to a successful job. I find high-school students' enthusiastic tales of volunteer activities edifying. Many students serve others and the environment while learning valuable life skills and lessons, based on the interconnectivity of our humanity. They come to realize what they have to offer, which is sometimes a simple helping hand. Universities evaluate high-school students for their extracurriculars (including volunteering), GPA, SAT/ACT/AP tests, and the application process (including writing essays and interviews when available). I've encountered only a few students cynical about volunteering. Once Evan, a high-school freshman at the time, and I went to Rosewood Retirement Home in La Puente, he to play his sax and I my guitar. Evan played "Pink Panther," and with exaggerated, furtive steps, walked around the room, Ta-Dom, Ta-Dom. Funny, watching Evan perform, I flashbacked to Bill Clinton, enjoying a few moments of bliss, jamming away, playing his saxophone on the Arsenio Hall Show in 1992.

Patients were clapping, singing, swaying in their wheelchairs, some just as smoothly as those on their feet; the staff cheered and energized us. I played "Blowing in the Wind" on the guitar, and we all sang "You Are My Sunshine." A thin, bright-eyed woman sang the words perfectly. Elijah, a handsome man in his eighties, commented and applauded heartily as we all sang, "So exciting, music." He later sang a plaintive tune in Spanish; a few of the nurses had tears running down their cheeks. Such moments, though rare, light up a room. All were having a good time, and Evan and I were pleased the patients and staff enjoyed themselves. We had lots of fun. Alluding to the age-old maxim, Evan commented, "It's as satisfying to give, as it is to receive." Students participate in such activities as visiting older residents in a convalescent hospital; assisting teachers with young children; returning books to library shelves, handing out brochures at museums, and cleaning parks and ocean shores. Returning from a trip to Santa Monica Beach to pick up trash, a student poetically reported: "I'm not just picking up garbage like a robot, but enjoying the waves swishing over my feet, socializing, and soaking in the sun's rays." Another student told me: "I go to the ocean and my sorrows float into the sea." Teenagers approach many doors to adulthood. When the doors are opened, teenagers can walk through; adults must welcome their arrival with a well-designed, technologically-advanced education system, interlinked through the sharing of resources enabled by the Internet. I was talking with a small group of students about strategies to study/learn well, and they included volunteering as part of gaining life and work experience. Many of my students relate how they welcome mentoring opportunities. I encourage them to let friends and relatives know that they would like to be mentored. A student related that after a year volunteering at a golf club, he was offered a part-time paying job that he really appreciated and enjoyed. Some students asked about my volunteering in the United States and in Latin America. Just as my students, I've always enjoyed and benefited from volunteering, especially with Southern Mexico's street children and indigenous people.

****

Since its beginning, I've been loosely associated with Matraca, a service in Xalapa, Veracruz, Mexico, which was established in 1991 to serve working street children (some homeless). Sadly, there are about 180,000 children and adolescents who live in the streets of Mexico, 20,000 of them less than five years old. The U. N. reports more than 20,000 Mexican children are victims of sex trafficking. Matraca represents not only an actual institution, but also a metaphor for my own soul-searching and self-inquiry about poverty and malnutrition, in this case among the indigenous and working street children of Veracruz and Chiapas, Mexico. Though making progress in serving the malnourished worldwide, we continue to embrace the responsibility to aid the 195 million malnourished children, most living in sub-Saharan Africa and Asia. "Every year malnutrition contributes to at least one-third of the eight million deaths of children under the age of five (Doctors Without Borders)."

Matraca is an acronym for *Movimiento de Apoyo a Niños Trabajadores y de la Calle* (Movement to Support Children Workers and Street Children). But *matraca* also means "noise-maker," a wooden toy that Mexican children spin when they want to celebrate or play. It makes a clacking noise, representing the children's liveliness, spaciousness, and freedom to explore, discover, and play. Hooray! Whoopee! Yeah! Dance and whirl. Laugh the bliss of being alive.

Xalapa means "sandy waters" in the native language of Nahuatl. Xalapa is in the center of the state of Veracruz, ancestral land of the Olmecs, Totonacas, Chichimecas, Toltecas, Otomies, Popolucas, Mayas, Tzotzils, Chinateas and Teochichimecas. This birthplace of Mexico's pre-Hispanic cultures still softly whispers through ancient art and from deep within the eyes of indigenous descendants. The lonely jagged mountain peaks of Sierra Madre Oriental dominate the landscape of western Veracruz. Rolling green foothills unveil fields of yellow flowers, rich coffee beans, *animalitos*, and peaceful, loving people with some *bandidos* in the mix. In the gray-cool harbor of Veracruz, Hernán Cortez, *gran conquistador* of the Aztecs, plunked down his thundering permanent anchor in 1519. Now the state of Veracruz is a 450-mile stretch, a multi-ethnic-blended tapestry of seven million people, with a large indigenous population, Europeans, Afro-Caribbeans, and Africans. There are small immigrant communities of Lebanese, Basques, Italians, Spaniards, Greeks, French-Cubans and mostly friendly gringos. Some 3,000 years ago, the powerful and sophisticated Olmecs created their own mathematics, religious myths and calendar, which were later adopted by the Aztecs and the Mayans. The Olmecs were master carvers of giant basalt heads, nine to ten feet tall and nine to ten tons in weight, with large-lips and broad-noses and facial expressions of faint disapproval.

I viewed the port of Veracruz at a magical moment of sunrise: the barest light on hundreds of eager fishermen with hopes for an abundant catch, in boats pushing into the salty sea; waters gradually illuminated by pinks and oranges of the morning sun, dabbled hues on oil-rig-shadowed silvery water. Into the evening, lively marimba bands played in the park. People enjoyed *danzon*, *cervezas*, and fresh seafood. Children shrieked gleefully; a beggar was mesmerized by rhythmic-sensual dancing in the steamy plaza.

****

The working children of Xalapa pass hours in the streets selling gum, cleaning car windshields, and flagging down taxis. Some dress as clowns, juggling and entertaining for tips. They stay one step ahead of the *Seguridad Publica* whose officers attempt to remove them from the frenetic streets. Fortunately, most of the children maintain strong bonds with their families. In the 1990s, however, about 150 of Xalapa's three thousand working children had no home. One Easter week, I was at Matraca's downtown facility of classrooms, offices, medical dispensary, kitchen, and showers. Young teens, Salim, Luis, and Jose talked to me about how they managed their lives, finding shelter, sleeping on the streets, getting small jobs and begging, dreaming of having a special love, a happy family life and the opportunity to go to school. They kicked the *fútbol* and played basketball with other children in Matraca's outside patio. Drying off from a shower, another street-youngster, Ezekial Macial, popped his head out, wet hair over his eyes, like a seal emerging at sea-surface. At a nearby traffic intersection, Santiago Lopez, hoping for tips, was washing windshields. He later told me how he and four other youngsters were recently detained for three days as a traffic menace. "I was afraid and alone." I interviewed Mariana Muñoz who works in an agrarian movement with indigenous farmers desiring self-sufficiency, access to water, tools and quality seeds. Soledad Alvarez told me stories about the seven young girls and one six-year-old boy—all previously homeless— with whom she lived and cared for in Casa Matraca, a home on the outskirts of Xalapa. Esmeralda Ortiz described visiting working children on the streets. Armed with several related newspaper articles, Director Lázaro Luna outlined coordinated activism against a newly proposed law that would lower the penal age of young people from sixteen to fourteen. That night, at the cathedral celebration of *Sábado de Gloria,* lights of orange flames spread blessings to all, including the bent, chattering *ancianas,* selling sundries for pennies in the park across the cobbled-stone street. Better to pass on blessings with bright candles however small than "to curse the darkness."

A sixteen-year-old boy, Felipe Guzman, whom I've known since he was nine, was waiting outside of Matraca to talk with me. He had been abandoned, along with his sister, Angelita, when he was eight. Over the years, he would take advantage of a few of Matraca's services but preferred his independence. He didn't do well with rules, and both enjoyed and suffered from street life. His sister found a home with friends of her mother, but the stepfather was sometimes drunk and abusive, so she would flee for a while and live on the streets. I always looked forward to being with Felipe and, at times, his sister, learning about their lives, encouraging them to go to school with available scholarships from Matraca. Entrepreneurial and charismatic, he survived by guiding tourists, sometimes taking them to the unseemly pockets of town, known for drugs and prostitution. He used cheap inhalants to get high and warm himself. But this night, losing all sense of the hustle and cockiness he usually conveyed, he told me through tears about his seventeen-year-old sister, who worked as a prostitute for almost a year before committing suicide. "She despaired," he said bleakly. And then, long into a dark night, we exchanged stories, sobbed together; he at times raged like a mad wolf. We offered our loving feelings to a teenage girl killed by her own misery.

****

Talking to Felipe, I remembered Todd Goldman, my next-door neighbor on Beachwood Drive in Los Angeles during my last two years of high school. Todd and I were occasional basketball friends. Returning to my old neighborhood some six years later, I was saddened when Todd's mother told me he had taken his own life. "He didn't fit in; he felt unwelcome and became inward." It took a while but I accepted that Todd felt a relief from his suffering; I wish him peace to this day.

Todd was basketball crazy. To my mother's dismay, he would shoot hoops late into the night. Mom would get upset when she saw me shooting the basketball after dark on the weekends, rebounding, passing and shooting with Todd, a very special, probably too sensitive young man-boy. We adults don't always sense our children's very unique needs as they are growing, and sometimes we don't understand what's going on within them. Todd's attentive and caring parents and family perhaps never fully appreciated the pressure and dark moments Todd suffered during his high-school days. I know I didn't.

I reminisced about Todd and the respect he had for basketball and the excitement we both felt playing and practicing. We couldn't wait to get into a game at the public courts, and experience those unexpected moments "in the zone." Basketball energized his imagination and gave him a sense of satisfaction. We weren't stars, but were good enough most of the time to play on a pick-up team, 4-on-4 and 3-on-3 half court. Sometimes we'd play 5-on-5 full court. Finding the best available players hanging out, we'd shout, "We've got next," hoping to stay on the court for as many games as possible.

Todd, only of medium height, with a ridiculously terrible posture, and not the best eyesight, was scrappy and could, from hours of home practice, effectively shoot from long range; getting free, he'd launch a shot without hesitation. Todd was best when our team would rebound well and make a quick pass outside where he would go for three or four in a row, always moving, lots of energy, "money in the bank." His jump shot from the top of the key was better than from the corners, as he practiced in a long but narrow driveway just outside my bedroom window; the basket was measured ten feet carefully, attached above the garage door. From the driveway, our fantasy took us to a sold-out Madison Square Garden. He and I spontaneously played out imaginary court scenarios: pick and roll, cut to the basket, screen, take a charge, switch from man-to-man to zone defense. Playing H-O-R-S-E, we were Wilt, Jerry West, Elgin Baylor, Bill Russell and Oscar Robertson. I thought of Todd when, while teaching at Bellarmine Prep in a 1969 charity game, faculty versus "stars," I actually played five minutes against a professional super-scorer, Rick Barry, sitting out the season's first thirty-two games to protest the relocation of the Oakland Oaks to Washington DC and becoming the Washington Caps. "If I wanted to go to Washington, I'd run for president," he grumbled.

Making up for a lack of physical intimidation, Todd could be vocal, loose with praise, "Yeah, baby"; criticism, "Gotta make that, man"; and instruction, "Block out." "Screen for me." Unlike at high school, on the basketball court he was well-liked and his hyper-chattering seemed to fit in. Black players thought he was cool. A good passer, he was smart and humble enough to feed better shooters, especially if he was "off." He was not a "hot dog," except when he was fooling around at home in his driveway with illusions of grandeur. Sometimes I'd hear him late at night, talking to himself: "Nice shot, man!" "You fouled me!" "No bed 'til 10 of 10 from the line." He wouldn't rub it in on the few occasions when our team won easily. He talked to me about what he learned from famous players who wrote books. "Do the basics in your sleep. . . . Adapt to your teammates on the court and adjust to the adversary whom you should always respect. . . . You're learning about life not just how to perfect your sport. . . . You and your opponent are not enemies, but potential friends learning sportsmanship, playing within basic rules of fairness. . . . Be a gracious loser even if you hate to lose. . . . Do the best to win but never if it entails intentionally injuring another player. . . . The goal is to compete as a team 'in the flow'; have fun, win or lose, keep improving. . . . Basketball like all sports has its artistic side exemplified in the greatest players who are in a world of their own. . . . They take you to another dimension. That's why Madison Square Garden and Boston Garden are cathedrals."

We practiced passing to each other in Todd's driveway: bounce passes, lob and chest passes, getting the ball inside or throwing a high pass over the defense. Todd, the first to point out to me that assists equal baskets, would pass behind his back and through a defender's legs, not to show off but when he needed to. He made skilled players look better by reading their body language and matching their rhythm in passing and receiving the ball in stride, just at the right speed, height, and angle. His weakness was that he couldn't rebound with the big guys. After taking a few sharp elbows to the ribs, he shied away from an inside game. He bonded with tall, muscular players who could jump and make strong outlet passes. Our strategy was to find at least one big man to rebound and deliver passes to Todd, this awkward guy swishing long jump shots. Occasionally opposition team players, as happens to most successful shooters, intentionally fouled Todd hard, knocking him to the ground; he surprised me with his toughness, telling me he always felt the physical aches *after* the game.

Sometimes, waiting for a game, or in his driveway, we would just hang out. He liked to sit on the basketball, which I'd tell him was not good for it. He'd just laugh and talk about the Lakers. Todd rarely expressed his inner feelings, a reticence we shared. But when he confided to me about his emotions on a few occasions, it was a deep exchange. He told me he felt clumsy and unpopular in high school; he spoke too loudly or withdrew, painfully self-conscious. Girls avoided him and laughed at his poor complexion. He would turn red when he had to speak to a girl at school. On a few occasions, classmates shouted anti-Semitic remarks at him. I'm reminded as a parent and teacher to be aware of young people who are under stress, who may feel bullied or ostracized. Suicide is rare for children, but increases dramatically in adolescence. According to the Centers for Disease Control and Prevention (CDC), suicide is the third leading cause of death for 15 to 24 year olds. Boys are four times more successful in completing suicide because they tend to use more lethal means—firearms, jumping, and hanging—than girls, who cut themselves and overdose more frequently.

****

Matraca continues to serve street and homeless children and teens; it celebrated its tenth anniversary in 2001, highlighted by a visit from Bishop Samuel Ruiz, who defended the human rights of Mexico's indigenous, especially in Chiapas, Mexico's southernmost state. He was fluent in Tzotzil and Tzeltal, the region's two most important native languages and served for forty years in Chiapas before he resigned on his 75th birthday on November 3, 1999. When I think of this friend of the poor, I'm reminded of the thirteenth-century Persian, Muslim poet, Rumi: "I'm so small, I can barely be seen. How can this great love be inside me? Look at your eyes: they're small, but they see enormous things." The social philosophy of inclusion born in the Mexican Revolution, some one-hundred years ago, still reverberates in leaders such as Samuel Ruiz: sharing of land and resources; dignified work; appreciation for indigenous cultures, religions, and customs; nurturing and educating children; and replacing the exploitation of the poor with broad fair-trade policies.

Chiapas has a population of four million, and is a land of spectacular flowers, lakes, plants, rivers, hills, volcanoes, thick jungles, and forests producing mahogany and rosewood. Tourists visit the Mayan archaeological sites of Palenque, Bonampak, Izapa, and Yaxchilan. On a cool, lightly raining evening, I was in Parque Central de San Cristobal, Chiapas. The Mexican Marine Corps, snappily uniformed and accompanied by a full orchestra and chorus, were singing their hearts out: operatics and ballads of the Revolution such as "Adelita" (a woman with long black hair to whom the returning heroic revolutionary will make passionate love). The park was packed, yet children still found space to gleefully jump as the choir's full voice shook a giant banner illustrating two doves kissing, perched in the blue skies. *Todos a la Feria de la Primavera y de la Paz.* Festival of Spring and Peace. Lively violins, candies, popcorn, steamed corn on the cob, dancing, flirting. *Esperanza.* Hope for peace and well-being.

Hector Bustamante, lawyer and Jesuit scholastic, drove me to visit Acteal and Las Abejas, a peaceful group of Tzotzil Indians organized in 1992. We drove winding roads in a Nissan pickup. At times along lush green forests, people were scurrying with wood tied to their backs or pushing goats. Las Abejas[2] community in Acteal are "displaced," peaceful activists, organizing for social justice, a community mourning because of the massacre on December 22, 1997 of forty-five of their members in a murderous attack which lasted from 11:30 a.m. to 6:00 p.m. Juan Manuel Mercado, secretary of the Acteal community, showed me the makeshift chapel where many of the community were killed as they were praying and fasting for peace. Some fled into the hilly gorges; a pregnant young woman was stripped, violated, and her baby cut from her womb. Forty-five bodies are buried in two layers inside a concrete structure. Juan Manuel pointed out pictures of the deceased, including those of his mother and sister, affixed to the wall of the edifice. We sat and prayed quietly for ten minutes. Tears could not hide. Precious Rosita, now holding hands tenderly with Grandma, was one of the fifty orphaned, blinded from a paramilitary's bullet to the head.

After visiting Acteal, we ventured into the mountains to honor and take part in a wake for Clemente, a community friend. Our Nissan pickup at

---

[2]   http://acteal.blogspot.com/2007/12/acteal-ni-borrn-ni-cuenta-nueva.html

times slid backwards, a newly purchased coffin sticking out diagonally in the back. A few dusty horses stared at us as we approached the grieving community, some weeping, standing around the corpse of their Clemente—friend, relative, husband and father. He was only fifty-two years old. Hector wryly whispered, "He died of poverty." Many men wore white tunics. Celebrating Clemente's life, three men played a tender, plaintive elegy on a violin, guitar, and harp. The blanket-covered corpse was placed in the wooden coffin with some of Clemente's belongings and a few peso coins. We smelled the dreaded odor of death, but cherished the life and humanity surrounding it. Before we left, members of Victoriano's family offered us corn tortillas with beans, cooked over an open fire. They tasted *muy rico*, as we stood eating, offering condolences, smoke in our faces.

****

I visited a family in Miahuatlán. The giant domed church, with a three-tiered bell tower, hovers over the small homes. Because the young adults fled to the cities or the border, mostly older people and children remained. Two hundred of Miahuatlán's population of four thousand journeyed across the border to join the eleven million native-born Mexicans who live in the United States. People told me they were forced to leave because manufacturing, oil producing, fishing, raising sugar-cane, beans, bananas, and coffee did not employ or pay enough. A young teen with early onset cerebral palsy ran a mobile stand selling candy, cigarettes, and newspapers. She was wearing a pretty pink and white dress. A customer asked her to demonstrate that a lighter she was selling worked, but she couldn't quite manage. Spontaneously, seemingly out of nowhere, a swarthy young man swept the lighter out of her hand and skillfully struck a flame to satisfy her nodding, approving customer.

****

Invited to the 1998 Congress for Indigenous People, April 13–15 in Mexico City, I knew I was in for an adventure. Fifty-six different ethnic groups were represented, comingling and peacefully marching for human rights. Large groups gathered on the Zócalo for four days and three nights, thousands of indigenous people living in open tents on this *gran plaza* of *México Viejo*. Serendipitously, I camped out with them on this magical and massive square. The Zócalo (*Plaza de la Constitución*) is Mexico City's historic site for demonstrations, patriotic ceremonies, political speeches, the launching of the New Year, cultural celebrations, parades, and people meeting, or simply passing by. Lying close to the archeological ruins of Moctezuma's *Templo Major*, the sinking Metropolitan Cathedral has a strong presence. Watching the impressive gathering of animated, peaceful "citizens" were heavily-armed soldiers and tanks. Officials detained some foreigners to be deported. No-nonsense military officers confiscated one of my recyclable Kodaks, but I had another hidden in my back pocket. A family adopted me on the plaza so I could blend into the scene. There were marches and peaceful protests against economic oppression of Indian laborers and peoples. I heard mysterious languages: Tarahumara, Chol, Mixteco, Nahuatl, Zogue, Zapoteco, and the much more familiar Spanish. Feeling invisible, I took in the scene. Banners flew, greens, reds, whites of the Mexican flag: *Dignidad para los Indigenos* and *Nunca mas un México sin Nosotros*. "Dignity for Indigenous People. No more Mexico without us. We are also Mexico."

Outside the tents strewn across the plaza, small groups talked into the morning before sleeping between blankets insulating against the cold, stone-blocked plaza. We imagined golden Aztec temples and bright-feathered priests dancing on tops of pyramids. Valuing human life above all, this gathering of indigenous people inspired a new, far reaching and non-violent manner of human sacrifice.

4

Relax

*Never regard study as a duty,
but as the enviable opportunity to learn to
know the liberating influence of beauty in the
realm of the spirit for your own personal joy
and the profit of the community
to which your later work belongs.*
—Albert Einstein

How we feel about ourselves and our society influences our learning. High-school students are encouraged to pay attention to what matters for them individually, socially, and spiritually. High school is a time for an honest effort in multiple subjects to gain experience, learn one's potential, and begin to specialize based on individual interests and strengths. Students likewise learn skills of stress relief, using various ways to honor the body's need for rest and recreation.

I was very fond of a Special Ed teacher and consultant, friend Wells Longshore. Stricken with MS, he died in 1998. He and I shared teaching ideas for a few years early in our careers. We sought to balance the demand for our students to work hard, but at the same time learn how to relax. Wells thought it was vital to re-create oneself, practice tranquility, and sleep well in order to nurture ideas gestating below the level of consciousness. Focusing attention and relaxation are two sides of the same coin. Wells taught the students to calm and center themselves using simple breathing techniques. He lectured, "We can slow down so we are completely in the here and now to receive new learning as well as rest." Wells and I discussed the subject of stress, and how a student—just like an athlete—achieves the most success when he or she is able to concentrate in a relaxed way. On June 3, 2012 I saw Tiger Woods, intense-relaxed-focused, chip in an impossible shot: mind, eyes, hands and golf ball in the cup at the same moment.

At a later stage of his disease, a wheelchair-bound Wells visited his former Special Education students. They swarmed him affectionately, saying, "Now you are one of us." Wells received his PhD from Michigan State University, had been a spectacular ladies' man and displayed quite a temper on the basketball court in our younger days. He spent his last years in Spokane, Washington. A fanatic for the Gonzaga University basketball team, he went to most practices, still teaching players to breathe, focus and deliver. Athletes, students, parents, all benefit from such advice. Wells must have been beaming from the cosmos when the Gonzaga Bulldogs were ranked number one in the nation at the end of regular play in March 2013. The team adopted him as much as he embraced them.

Wells—always quick to find and promote the special gifts of his students—would have loved the January 15, 2012, *60 Minutes* segment, called "Jake." Jake, 13 and a sophomore in college, is one in ten million, an autistic savant, blessed with prodigious memory, who can conquer the most challenging memory tests. With Jake, it's not just the amazing ability to absorb and retain knowledge, it's the gift to contemplate and practice in the fields he loves: math, astronomy, and physics. "My mind is constantly buzzing with new theories. I would not have gotten so far without my autism." He is ambitious, eager to discover a groundbreaking extension of the Theory of Relativity. Jake can gobble up information at a rate that baffles most of us. His story is as much about healing as it is learning, and about outstanding parents who encourage uninhibited curiosity and exploration, which give meaning and direction. For fun, he memorizes the infinite series of the number known as *pi*. Feeling no sense of burden, no stress, he says he likes to analyze the logic in mathematics. In physics he explores light moving through cables, his lab walls filled with photographs of the cosmos. His dad said Jake at a young age slipped "from our world into a world of his own." He and his wife started noticing Jake was not happy unless "he was doing what he loved. Then he began to communicate." Realizing Jake's skills improved by doing what fired him up, his parents supported him. Jake enjoys tutoring others in math and science; he laughs when people tell him they are math and science phobic. His dad relates that when he walks on campus with the popular Jake, it's like walking with Elvis. He plans to graduate at age 14 and begin his PhD.

****

Wiping her brow, a high-school junior detailed how stressful school life can be: AP classes, an "awkward" social life, demanding parents. She felt nervous that people would make fun of her when called to offer her opinion in class. "I'm changing classes so I won't have to speak in front of the class. How can I get over being so self-conscious?" Students and parents have talked to me about pressure as they go through the high-school process, and how they cope with it. Stress is the way our bodies/minds respond to any challenge—be it positive, negative, big, or small. In extremely alarming conditions, various bodily defenses arise, a natural survival reaction meant for life-menacing situations. What we perceive or anticipate to be hostile activates the brain to stimulate the adrenal glands, which release hormones into the blood. Sometimes our perception tricks us into feeling threatened, our bodies reacting accordingly yet unnecessarily. We can wear ourselves out with excessive worry and anxiety. Negative emotional stress should not be prolonged or left undefined. It is vital to find ways to get things off our chests: confiding feelings to a friend; releasing emotions constructively through music, media, or exercise; taking breaks; having fun; re-charging and re-creating ourselves. When we inevitably make mistakes, we shouldn't dwell so much on what we may have done or not done, but dust ourselves off and move on hopefully wiser. Students tell me of the struggle sometimes to be oneself in high school and to say *no* amidst peer pressure to experiment with drugs and sex. Stress accompanies the journey of self-discovery for the high-school student. How we deal with it makes all the difference in the world. We need to be emotionally sound as well as intellectually sharp.

****

Learning about the power of the unconscious, teens are becoming aware they are building memories under the surface of their minds. They realize flashbacks don't just occur in movies but in the emotional texture of their lives. Educators and parents teach teens the importance of harmonizing the conscious and unconscious mind. The unconscious mind possesses valuable knowledge, and continuously learns "beneath the surface." Jung wrote that events not consciously noted still remain subliminally accessible below the threshold of consciousness. We can mine the depths of the collective unconscious, giving value to our lives, because of its evolving genetic wisdom surpassing our individual knowledge. Once a high-school sophomore told me she had a transcendent experience, a sense of joy and accomplishment after performing three "artistically and technically amazing" pieces at a violin recital. "The golden age of Beethoven became present in my own consciousness. Playing violin, I was lifted up into the holy company of past genius, and what was there? Just the plaintive, timeless, soulful music of the violin on transfixed ears."

What we see and learn unconsciously can later be brought into the conscious mind. Personable raconteur and noted physicist, Leonard Mlodinow writes in his book, *Subliminal*, that our conscious and unconscious determine how we view ourselves, and that we all have the basic desire to feel good about ourselves. Teachers and parents, aware of the original, inviolable inner goodness of their children, want them to feel happy. "Unconscious minds are active, purposeful and independent" (*Subliminal*). The unconscious possesses knowledge that is critical for our evolutionary survival. Opening up to new experiences, teens become more sensitive to non-verbal communication through body language. *Educare* is Latin, meaning *to draw out* the best potential in each student.

A student noted after an intense family argument that conflict never really ends until there is forgiveness, a breaking of the chain of defending, arguing with emotionally hurtful language, and paying each other back for being hurt. "There's so much stress when our family fights; it's not so easy to let go. I get hurt emotionally, and I feel the need to pay back my attacker." John Gottman, author of *The Seven Principles of Making Marriage Work*, writes that it takes five positive interactions (for example, listening, showing interest, asking sincere questions, being kind, and empathetic) to make up for one negative interaction (such as anger, sarcasm, fault finding, being judgmental, condescension, hostility, prejudice). Empathy is the foundation of the Golden Rule, not to do unto others what you do not wish done unto you. We all need forgiveness from time to time and probably, if we're honest, fairly often. If we need forgiveness for ourselves, with our myriad mistakes, we can give it as well. It is unhealthy to carry hate within.

Bamboo Bending

****

A tall girl with shoulder-length black hair entered the classroom in shock. She said her mom was on her way to pick her up. In a whisper, she said she lost a high-school classmate who was hit by a car in a crosswalk and killed. I had just heard about it from other students. A small group of shocked and heartbroken students gathered and consoled the girl and each other. The students hugged and cried. After about an hour, their parents picked them up or they walked or drove home. I saw the tender side of the teens, their naturally compassionate side. Parents and teachers want to protect our children from trauma, but sometimes we are helpless.

A few years ago, a high-school student was doing a paper on the subject of death and dying. Knowing I taught "Mental Fitness" at a hospital-hospice, she interviewed me. It was a strikingly odd combination: a youthful, vivacious teen asking about death. She soulfully reflected about caring for Grandma in home hospice. "To be with her, attend to her needs, sing to her, hold her hand, love her, and keep her warm and comfortable. Then she's just gone." Teachers often implore the students not to waste time. All is passing: *Don't miss your precious chance, only you can live your life.* When my mother was dying she told me: "Go for what you deeply need; now I can die in peace because I love life, even now, in my time of dying. Life itself is a gift to be lived until the end; and even with difficult and heartbreaking times, it includes happiness, exploration and fulfilling experiences." As the Italian saying goes, "May death find you fully alive!"

****

Within an hour of the announcement of the seven Challenger astronauts' tragic death on January 28,

1986, my mother revealed that doctors gave her three months to live. She gracefully accepted the results of the biopsy and her "terminal" prognosis. Yet she also spoke out, feeling humiliated and angry at what she perceived as poor, insensitive hospital care. I told her: "Let's go home." My sister Mary, with whom she was living, was eager to make her comfortable. After work, I would visit with her late into the cool evenings. A kind and efficient nurse, Felicia, stayed with Mom. She died on March 24th, three days after her birthday. "Why does this dying have to take so damn long?" she moaned a few days earlier.

All of us—even doctors, therapists, teachers, monks, rabbis, imams and priests—struggle with our "demons" and subtle preconceptions regarding death. I remember a Buddhist monk once telling me how he was unaffected by his mother's death, that he could easily just let her go. Yet welling in his eyes were tears. Perhaps he felt it was "proper" as a monk not to show grief, but the body does not lie. We are human beings first. In the movie *A Beautiful Mind*, John Nash tells his delusional voices and hallucinations that he won't talk to them anymore, that he feels the presence of their demand, but that he will not give them any more energy. Likewise, our spiritual efforts give us a peaceful detachment from the afflictive emotions that arise when facing the death of others and that of our own. Such emotions of dread, fear, anger, sorrow, habitual reactions, and compulsions may not go away, but if they have lost mastery over our souls, we can accept death as a natural process.

My mother was confident she was going beyond human existence into other dimensions of the conscious stream of light and life. She would be with her husband in a golden heaven with Jesus. She was going to be in a beautiful, unspeakable rapture, the beatific vision, the shining face of her God, eternal resurrection, the final destination. Usually, Mom could see right through me, so any solicitous attitude on my part was quickly dropped. Without any agenda, I felt we were simply together moment by moment. I'd help naturally without any preconceived ideas. As hospice work taught me, listening and being oneself—being there and not trying too hard—while being alert and of practical assistance, were the most helpful dispositions.

Mom and I seldom hugged warmly, but we shared a stimulating conversational closeness. She had a marvelous capacity for probing repartee and a broad appreciation of the arts. We talked about movies, TV shows, newspaper articles, sports, gardening, psychology, advice columns, politics, literature, and Catholicism. Mom taught me the art of an intellectual conversation, achieving a modicum of satisfactory closure by thinking something through and understanding the important questions. We recalled the rainy weekend afternoons when I was young, asking each other about our favorite things and *Huckleberry Finn*. Is this life only a beginning, a past journey leading to a new life? I can never answer this question for sure. This gift of human life is mystery enough. Like Einstein and a boy gazing at endless skies, in gratitude for being alive, I wonder and bow to Nature's beauty beyond any words.

One night, as if presented with a disconcerting puzzle, Mom had a perplexed look on her face. She was lost, talking to herself, frightened by hallucinations. Not knowing where the words came from, I said, "Those are experiences as you go deeper into the vast light of God. Relax. Let go. You're safe in the loving hands of your source and destiny." I matched my breath with hers, inhaling separately yet together, blessing her with every exhalation until she fell asleep.

I asked Mom: "Is there anything bothering you? Do you have any worries?" She said everything was all right. The pain in her body was intense at times. "It's difficult, Mom?" She'd nod her head yes and squeeze my hand tightly. One night Mary bought expensive French champagne for Mom. We celebrated her life with food, drink, TV, and conversation. She commented, "We are having a ball. . . . It's all just so ridiculous." At three in the morning, she asked me to sing a Gregorian chant. *Kyrie Eleison … Kyrie Eleison … Christe Eleison … Christe Eleison*, a spiritual lullaby. Lord have mercy on us; Christ have mercy on us. She closed her eyes and fell asleep.

Mom told me how hard it was for her family during the Depression. She worked in the competitive fashion field at a young age when it was a man's world in New York City. Even an ambitious, talented young woman could get discouraged at times. As feminine as you might feel, you had to be thick-skinned, lucky, and on your game to survive. I asked if she forgave me for not becoming a lawyer like her husband, my dad, and instead followed my dream of teaching. She told me she learned to forgive, but that, of course, there were some regrets. She not only wanted me to be an attorney, but also more traditionally Roman Catholic. She said I seemed happy and enthused about teaching, learning, and traveling to Central America and Mexico. She shed rare tears saying I was her favorite conversation partner. "Follow your own lights, no matter what I think you should be." I was humbled by her humanity and hard-earned wisdom. Mom would ask me to read to her. She loved a story from the Jewish tradition of Tashlich: One Tashlich—the afternoon of the first day of Rosh Hashanah, when everybody walks down to the river to symbolically throw the year's sins into the water, a sixty year old congregant started to cry. He had been unemployed for two years, profoundly resentful. No one would give much attention to his resume because of his age, he told anyone who asked. "I was throwing my bits of bread into the water like everyone, and I was thinking this is what society has always done to me, just thrown me down a river.... Yet suddenly I comprehended the verse 'Cast your sins into the depths of the sea.' And I started to cry, because I realized that I'd been throwing in everyone's sins but my own. My sin, I saw for the first time, was this endless bitterness. And it was time to cast it into the sea."

At the time I had a job through Baldwin Park Unified School District at a facility for men with mental challenges from schizophrenia to severe depression. Mom had always asked me about Adult Special Education. I told her of the teachers, students, and administrators who put together interesting and effective programs which served special needs students. "How do you describe a schizophrenic, Morgan?" I responded: "Confused. Disoriented. Fragmented. Hearing Voices. Here, then there, vacant, a mind disordered. Ideas disconnected. Intelligence and energy gone awry."

Mom replied: "Sometimes that's what dying is like. It just comes so fast, this dying." Yes, like a thief in the night.

****

Relax

Not Christian or Jew or Muslim, not Hindu,
Buddhist, Sufi or Zen. Not any religion or
cultural system. I am not from the East or the
West, not out of the ocean or up from the
ground, not natural or ethereal, not composed
of elements at all. I do not exist, am not an
entity in this world or the next, did not
descend from Adam and Eve or any origin
story. My place is placeless, a trace of the
traceless. Neither body or soul . . . I know, first,
last, outer, inner, only that breath breathing,
human being.
—Rumi

Watching the Chinese coach of the 2012 gymnastic team, passing Buddhist prayer beads through his fingers as his players warmed up, I thought of Chinese Buddhist friends who likewise use prayer beads, offer incense, and participate in Buddhist rituals from their Chinese culture. They go to the temple to honor ancestors as well as participate in religious holidays. Some chant *sutras* and serve at the temple or volunteer at a hospital. All religions have different rituals and doctrines, but the essential teachings of compassion, wisdom, and living respectfully and justly with others are embodied in all of them. Different practices and ideas may seem foreign to us, just as our own religious beliefs and rituals may appear odd to others. Once I asked a Chinese friend at the Rosemead Buddhist Monastery about his custom of burning ceremonial money, paper gold bars, and a paper model of a Mercedes-Benz. Entering the Temple of Ancestors, he mindfully presented a food offering for his departed, beloved grandfather. He said it was a gesture of respect, common in Chinese culture, acknowledging a life now ended. "Grandpa would have loved to have had a Benz; I'm not being literal. Our thoughts of loving kindness for him are expressed in a ritual. We are remembering his kindness and vitality, showing our appreciation. In a sense, Papa is not dead for us." I now understood this meaningful ritual, and I became not only comfortable but also gained value from this perspective. I sometimes go to the Rosemead Buddhist Temple and pay my respects to my Chinese father-in-law whose picture is in the Temple of Ancestors. After a deep reconnection with my own Catholic religious tradition, I began to feel an empathy with Chinese Buddhist practices such as honoring our ancestors.

****

When I find myself in times of trouble,
Mother Mary comes to me,
speaking words of wisdom,
let it be . . . .
—Lennon-McCartney

Entering the Rosemead Buddhist Temple, I sometimes stop a few moments by the white statue of Quan Yin, soaking in her serene-faced embrace of the children of Earth. The statue is not an idol representing some being "out there"; it is an aesthetic figure pointing to a compassionate consciousness, a mythic representation that encourages us to be kind to ourselves and others. I have similar sentiments when I view images of the Virgin of Guadalupe. Quan Yin began to make sense to me as it reminded me of my Catholic tradition. In Mexico City and San Miguel de Allende, I witnessed the Black Mother honored with a procession through the crowded streets, her statue colorfully dressed, celebrated with songs, music and flowers. There is a variety of "Black Mothers": the Black Madonna in Europe, Kali for Hindus, Tara in Tibetan Buddhism and Crow Mother among the Hopi Indians. She inspires pilgrims and protesters who seek freedom from oppression. Closer to home, some years ago I arrived early at Our Lady of Lourdes, in East Los Angeles, for the Festival of Black Madonna, the Dark Mother, *Madre Morena*, Lover of the Poor, the Compassionate One. I watched Alessandra Belloni and her ensemble from Southern Italy practice the hour or so before the sacred rite began. Alessandra sang, danced and played the *tamburello*, a white framed drum. Tambourines, frame drums, and percussion instruments accompanied her. Melodies were soulfully vibrating through the room: *Canto della Madonna di Montevergine*, praising Mother Earth; *Ave Maria*, a jubilant, plaintive song; a Brazilian Yoruba processional chant honoring the Goddess of Love; the *Ritmo e Danza*, from Calabria, sung during the Middle Ages as protection from the plague and fear of death. Alessandra was then perhaps sixty years old, with a graceful body, and a haunting, powerful voice. Her long black hair flowed down her white summer dress, embroidered with pink blossoms. She performed a wild ecstatic dance, a healing trance, called the *tarantella* by women who worked the fields in southern Italy. Often exploited and abused, the women danced to conquer the hurt from the "bite of the tarantula," or the "bite of love," releasing their feelings of anger and resentment, as well as repressed sexual frustrations and desires. After her masterful performance, Alessandra was at the entrance saying good-bye. I felt I wanted to greet her, but people were so tightly crowded around, I just waved and cheered. In the distance, I could see smoke in the San Gabriel Valley; houses and forests were burning in wind-blown blazes. Our Mother can be fierce and merciless as well, with a mind of Her own.

****

Bamboo Bending

Profound, peaceful, unfabricated, translucent,
uncreated, this reality I have found is like
an elixir of immortality.
—Shakyamuni Buddha

In 1961 I was a high-school junior, boarding as a student-worker at Loyola High School in Los Angeles. During the summer and some weekends, I would hitchhike around L.A., not always having a definite destination in mind: Venice Beach, downtown, Hollywood & Vine, the Farmer's Market, the San Fernando Valley, and the Fairfax District. Once, just above the frenetic 101 freeway, I was attracted to an Indian Vedanta temple, the Hollywood Hills' miniature version of the Taj Mahal. On a bright, blue-sky day, the Southern California sun shone on the yellow domes of the white, gold-spired temple. Built in 1938 by the Vedanta Society of Southern California, it attracted Westerners interested in Eastern mysticism and philosophy, including literary luminaries Aldous Huxley and Christopher Isherwood. The society's goal was "to promote harmony between Eastern and Western thought." Inside the temple, I contemplated an artistic depiction of Buddha's round face, peaceful and tender, across from the Shroud of Turin's image of Jesus. I just sat there, a bit uncomfortable at first, then gradually relaxed, enjoying the still sanctuary. I felt guilty, having been raised a strict Catholic; but on subsequent occasional visits, I could slow down, reflect, and escape the ordinary anxieties of a high-school student.

I associate Buddhism with the serene Shakyamuni sitting in meditation, peaceful and full within. Though meditation is not for everyone, I have found it can be one means to cope with and understand everyday stress. I am better able to control my reactions to thoughts and soften harsh judgments, even if the thoughts and emotions are unsettling. Buddhists sometimes call meditation "stopping the chatter of the mind." Buddhism attracted me as a philosophy of meditation and source of psychological wisdom, but never as a religious organization that I wished to join formally. Monks, just as priests, rabbis, ministers, and imams, can practice earnestly or become mediocre, and, at extremes, even abusive and financially exploitive. I've grown more skeptical of religious organizations, but encouraged by the human spirit that is found in real practitioners and communities of various traditions, including secular humanism.

****

I have stopped forever
doing violence to beings.
—Shakyamuni Buddha

(Steve) Jobs' love of simplicity in design was
honed when he became a practitioner of
Buddhism. . . . Daniel Kottke said,
"Zen was seen in his whole approach of stark,
minimalist aesthetics, intense focus."
—Walter Isaacson

For forty-five years, the Buddha (the awakened one) communicated his illuminated state and the means to attain it. He never said he was a god, but that he was "awake," and, crossing and re-crossing the Indian plains, began to teach wisdom and compassion to monks and lay people, men and women. He proposed a way to end unnecessary mental-emotional suffering: cultivating moral integrity and empathy; learning meditation to gain insight about thoughts, intentions, and acts that make us suffer and those which lead to happiness. Neither embracing an extremely ascetic existence nor a greedily self-indulgent one, Buddha acquired liberation through the "Middle Way." He counseled his disciples to pay attention to their physical being: sit up straight, walk, notice, breathe and feel alive. Witnessing mind, body and emotion, one can directly experience all that arises in consciousness: physical states, sensations accompanying the breath, feelings, and thoughts, the awareness of the complex movement of energy within each person.

People from varying religions (or without any religion) practice forms of private and group Buddhist meditation. In Westwood's Hammer Museum, Diana Winston (director of mindfulness education at UCLA's Mindful Awareness Research Center) guides weekly meditations to "pay attention to present moment experiences with openness, curiosity and a willingness to be with what is." UCLA neurologist Rick Hanson and neuropsychologist Richard Mendius (www.wisebrain.org) propose in their book, *Buddha's Brain*, to identify "the brain states underlying the mental states of happiness, love, and wisdom, and how you can use your mind to stimulate and strengthen these positive brain states." The Dalai Lama commented that Western psychology has overemphasized negative emotions such as anger, greed, and excessive selfishness. Buddhism, as do other great traditions, offers ways to open the mind and heart to create well-being. Buddha asked for questions and welcomed conversations, telling his disciples to test his teachings according to his or her own good sense, not just to follow because "Buddha says." Sometimes, he would refer the seeker to another teacher or ask him to return to his former teacher.

A person is not a separate entity but a relational coming together of the body's life-force, sensations, perceptions, intentions, and consciousness. The dynamic interplay between mind and body is as inseparable as is one human being from all humanity. Living in a local and global community, we are interwoven as a blanket of stars in immense, dark skies. Indian philosopher and teacher, Jiddhu Krishnamurti, reflects on the heart of meditation: "What is important in meditation is the quality of the mind and the heart. It is not what you achieve, or what you attain, but rather the quality of a mind that is innocent and vulnerable. Wander by the seashore and let this meditative quality come upon you. If it does, don't pursue it. What was is the death of what is. Or when you wander in the hills, let everything tell you the beauty and the pain of life, so that you awaken to your own sorrow and to the ending of it."

****

Chinese religion is so different from Western belief systems that some experts have argued that for most of their history, the Chinese have been a people little concerned with the spiritual. Nothing could be more wrong. Up until the twentieth century, China was a land imbued with religion and the spiritual. It wasn't rooted in and controlled by powerful institutions like a church with a clergy but instead consisted of a system of daily practices, including ancestor worship, veneration of mountains and streams, worship of famous people or local gods, belief in fate and fortune-telling, and techniques of physical cultivation like tai chi and qigong.
—Ian Johnson (*Wall Street Journal*)

The practices of Confucianism and Daoism were widespread throughout China at the time Buddhism was introduced. Located above the central plains, Song Shan was home to the Daoists' Zhongyuc Temple, the Confucians' Songyang Academy and the Buddhists' Shaolin Monastery. With funds from Emperor Xiaowen of the Northern Wei Dynasty, the Shaolin Monastery was established in 495 CE by Abbot Bao Tuo, a Buddhist monk who came from India.

Bodhidharma (Chinese name, Da Mo), according to legend, traveled to Henan province where the sacred Song Shan Mountain looms over the Yellow River. It was thirty years after Bao Tuo had established Shaolin Temple, when Bodhidharma requested but was refused permission to stay at the Shaolin Monastery. Bodhidharma, an Indian prince who became a Buddhist monk, began teaching in silent meditation. Da Mo quickly became famous, and Emperor Wu invited him to the palace where they talked about Buddhism until the emperor heard what he didn't want to hear.

Emperor Wu: Are my actions of building many temples and statues praiseworthy?

Da Mo: No.

Emperor: Is the Buddha in the world?

Da Mo: No.

The emperor ran the serene Da Mo out of the palace.

Climbing high into the mountains, Bodhidharma meditated for nine years; he combined mental and physical discipline (kung fu) to sharpen concentration, self-control, and devotion. Then he was welcomed into Shaolin Temple, where he became the first Patriarch of Ch'an Buddhism, later transmitting, heart-to-heart, mind-to-mind, the enlightened lineage to his successor, a practice which would continue through the years.

Though today's scholars question whether Bodhidharma ever lived in the Shaolin Temple, the temple flourished until the fourteenth century when the rulers of the Qing Dynasty banned the Buddhist monk-soldiers. Devotions and practice went underground. Today one can visit the temple with its more than two hundred stone stupas, commemorating monks over the centuries. Monks from the Shaolin Temple teach kung fu and meditation in the San Gabriel Valley and around the world. Tao Wu Ti (502–549 CE) and four succeeding emperors encouraged Buddhists to build

Relax

shrines and temples in Northern China: a five-story temple with five tall bronze statues of Buddha; a forty-three foot Buddha using forty-nine tons of copper and five hundred tons of gold; and carved Buddhist shrines in the caves at Yungang and Longmen (with 97,000 statues), along the banks of the Yi River. By 515 CE almost 14,000 Buddhist temples were established in China. Buddhism's golden age was in the Tang period, (618–907 CE). Because Buddha insisted that he was not to be worshipped as a god, at first there were only artistic renditions of footprints, symbolizing impermanence and Buddha's presence and path to acquire transcendent wisdom. Wheels with eight spokes represented the eightfold path of wisdom (right understanding and thought), morality (right speech, action, livelihood), and concentration (right effort, mindfulness, focus) leading to enlightenment. Some common symbols were the lotus, jewels, and the left-facing swastika (also found in Hinduism, Jainism and early European history, meaning good fortune and well-being). The Nazis used a right-facing rotation to symbolize its evil regime. It wasn't until the first century that statues of Buddha appeared.

> *All life is interrelated. We are all caught in an inescapable network of mutuality tied into a single garment of destiny.*
> –Martin Luther King Jr.

My father-in-law, Papa Fu, one of Chiang Kai-shek's heroic pilots, embodied for me the best qualities of Chinese cordiality, family living, interest in learning and respectfulness. On July 26, 2012, Besse Cooper of Monroe, Georgia celebrated her 116th birthday with a party. Only seven others have reached 116 years old. Her secret: "I mind my own business." That was Papa Fu; he didn't want to bother anyone. He enjoyed his own life and didn't need to live his life through others.

Even when he was older, I would see him, smiling and with a brisk step, walk to the park to play tennis. I wrote the following to honor him when he died.

This morning just before light, January 17, 2001, my father-in-law, Papa Fu, passed away. His family gathered around his deathbed, believing that Papa's spirit would linger for some hours in the room. We talked to him, saying good-bye, *zaijian*, dear elegant long-limbed man. Touching him for the last time, we wept contemplating Papa's serene face. Happy that Papa was not suffering any longer in the body, I brought two friends, Buddhist monks Chao Chu and Dao Yuan, to be with Papa and comfort Ma and the family. I recalled how Papa, gracious and content, lived a peaceful and enjoyable life. I would visit with Papa at ten o'clock after teaching night school. Assisted by a metallic ventilator, Papa breathed fitfully through a pipe in his throat. There were moments of calm and acceptance as I cradled his head in my palm, holding and very gently massaging his wrapped, slender hands. At times, he instinctively tried to pull out the tubes invading his body. I'd put my face close to his and look into his loving eyes. Papa enjoyed writing and reading, so I read some favorite texts from Jewish, Sufi, Christian and Buddhist traditions, sending feelings of well-wishing to him, my desire that he be happy and tranquil. Who can say what awaits our final breath?

****

I urge students to think for themselves when it comes to religion. Some have been hurt by the negative side of religion, its cultism and the abuse of power found in all religions and politics. No religion, political institution or other person has the right to dominate one's discriminating ability to choose for oneself. It's vital we all reflect, criticize and feel for ourselves, especially when a person in holy robes is preaching in front of us. We must continue to speak up against those who misuse power, such as religious leaders who cover up child abuse, or condone abuse of women, or discriminate because of race or sexual orientation. As Sam Harris, atheist and author of *The End of Faith*, warns: we have to stand up to those who practice exclusion, intolerance, and "holy horrific" violence and war. As Harris rightly worries, if we fail to openly criticize dangerous elements within all religions and stay open to new scientific discoveries, we won't survive as a global community.

When someone disagrees with us about religion or rejects religion altogether, we should not react violently. Atheist Richard Dawkins talks about the importance of not disrespecting those with whom we differ. "If I go to a Hindu temple, I take off my shoes because I don't want to disrespect them." The philosopher Santayana wrote that skepticism is the chastity of the mind so we shouldn't sacrifice it too easily. Religion at its best teaches love and kindness, history, the Golden Rule, a sense of community, the ability to discriminate right from wrong, and how to be an involved citizen. Great religious traditions have mystical teachings and stories of individuals who convey testimonies, often poetic, of transcendent experience. In the '60s and '70s, although a Catholic, I ventured outside my cultural and religious upbringing and discovered Eastern meditation exercises and philosophy that complemented my Catholic tradition.

Several years ago I was angry at a God whom I felt sat in judgment of mankind, favoring some, annihilating others. I wondered if my conceptions of self as a separate soul or entity and God as a personal, parental, all-powerful being were flawed. Is, as Buckminster Fuller surmises, God a verb rather than a noun? Perhaps the idea of God as a judge that controls all, rewards and condemns is wrong? Bruce Hood writes

in *The Self Illusion: How the Social Brain Creates Identity*:
"You only exist as a pattern made up of all the other
things in your life that shape you.... This does not
mean that you do not exist at all but rather that you
exist as a combination of all the others who complete
your sense of self." Andrew Olendzki summarizes: "As
with every other aspect of the mind and body, the self
is an event that occurs rather than a thing that
exists.... We never just notice an object; we engage
with it emotionally."

****

> *Love cures people—both the ones who give it*
> *and the ones who receive it.*
> —Dr. Karl Menninger

All life is a learning experience. One of my former
students, Gloria Santiago, delved into psychology in
college, and asked me about teaching Adult Special
Education and working as a recreational therapist. She
was specifically interested in seeking advice about
problematic addictive behavior, as well as shame and
forgiveness. Gloria wanted me to share some of my
experiences working in the East Los Angeles mental
health clinic, where, as recounted earlier, I was
dramatically fired.

Many of us overindulge or binge to soften the pain
of a life crisis. While we affirmed the importance of
enjoying celebrations, good food and company, we
also warned our clients about the dangers of addictive
behavior, sometimes associating with gambling, sex,
alcohol, drugs, shopping and eating. It's not these
activities that are "wrong," but if they over-control us,
our cravings inevitably lead to ruin. Some of us have
to abstain from certain activities because once started,
we cannot stop. We all have unique tendencies, and
must practice self-control when appropriate. I am sure

many of us know someone who died from alcohol/drugs or whose lives/families were destroyed. A client said she stuffed herself with greasy "comfort food" to suppress the pain and hurt she felt in an abusive relationship. Wanting to live with a girlfriend, her husband left her. He would visit, staying a few days with his wife before returning to his girlfriend. She used alcohol and marijuana to relax, but, after "my total dependence on highs and feeling wasted, I'm seeking therapy. I want to be in the right state of mind to separate from a husband who always hurts me. Emotionally, I'm broken; my body is not healthy." There's no way out but to squarely face problems, and this client was very brave to do so. She was fidgety and manic when she began therapy, but slowly began connecting with the staff and other clients. Not wanting to feel judged by the therapists, she stated: "I don't want to be talked down to." She asked questions and decided to open up. She agreed that denial and desperate distraction through over-indulging prolonged her unresolved conflict with her abusive husband. She recounted childhood beatings from her parents, and became conscious of the sad, fearful, lonely feelings she was trying to suppress. Dampening those feelings, she would over-eat, staying awake for exaggerated hours, getting inebriated and passing out. She said, "I'm changing myself with your help."

Another client observed: "I'm saying *yes* when I mean *no*. I'm afraid to be rejected; I already feel bad about myself." Though an adult, she felt her life had to conform to inhibiting, parental voices which blocked a full life waiting to flourish. She struggled with inner, habitual voices: "I'm no good"—"I'm not worthy of love and respect"—"I have to be a *good* girl"—"You're no good"—"It's your entire fault." I encouraged the client to slow down in order to take a more relaxed and objective view. She was evaluated by the therapeutic team, and then offered therapies to heal the physical-emotional hurting, while at the same time, addressing immediate needs. As the client calmed down, inner belittling voices faded into the background. Clients progressed through drug therapy, therapeutic processes and supporting relationships; they became aware of the life, intelligence, talent, and heart they were yearning to express.

****

> *I'm never going to forgive that degraded, sick*
> *bastard who raped me.*
> *He's no longer a human being.*
> —client who eventually
> forgave her violator

A therapist facilitates self-understanding and behavioral changes. Sometimes the therapist is rewarded by witnessing his client's positive evolution. I have observed a rape victim go through the process of forgiving a brutal perpetrator. If I were in her position, I don't know how I would react. How did this woman change into the forgiver of the man who violated her? "I'm not forgetting; I'm not being goody-goody. I'm giving up the hatred and revenge. I talk to the counselor and participate in group therapy so I can truly feel and observe my feelings. I integrate forgiveness into my multi-faceted personality." Erin Prizzey says: "I have been raped. It pollutes one's life. It is an experience that is contained within the boundaries of one's own life. In the end, one's life is larger. Assault by a stranger or within a relationship is very terrible. One is hurt, undermined, degraded, afraid. But one's life is larger." Recent remarks by Missouri Congressman Todd Akin, running for the US Senate in 2012, that "legitimate rape" rarely causes pregnancy horrified people with both its insensitivity and ignorance. Voters rejected Akin in his re-election bid.

Relax

*The most important thing in communication is
to hear what isn't being said.*
—Peter Drucker

Fritz Perls said that our most important "unfinished situations" will always emerge if we attentively participate in our own therapy. Therapy makes conflicts obvious and facilitates a natural process of completion. We encouraged clients to safely act out, move, exercise, be aware of bodily reactions (e.g., a "knot in the stomach," "a rigid neck"). Clients expressed feelings and some experienced positive emotional "catharsis" by letting go of troublesome "buried parts" of the self that take up excessive mental energy. Arthur Janov has written that early difficulties and trauma starting from life in our mother's womb have life-long consequences. We carry the history of all our experiences in our body-mind. Janov creates therapies to help clients re-live their painful experiences in order to release them.

One client felt shame and guilt for drunkenly abusing his wife. His parents had physically abused him as a child. In therapy, he put himself in the place of his wife. Two chairs were put in the middle of the group-therapy room. Imagining he was his wife, he spoke these words: "I'm happy to be your wife and I love you. But I'm not your mom." The client wept profusely, reminding me of Anthony Quinn's character Zampano in the movie *La Strada,* crying uncontrollably on the beach after realizing his cruelty to the only woman who loved him.

An episode of "The Twilight Zone" recounts the story of a family, a father and four children at Mardi Gras. The father was soon to die, and the children were excitedly looking forward to inheriting his riches. At the party, we witness the children's greed, envy, and jockeying for position with Dad. The father was aware of his children's motivations and the irony of everyone wearing a grotesque, gnarled mask. After the father died, the children could not remove their horrible masks, the true inner reality now molded for eternity onto their faces for all to see. Therapy allows us to be whole, to radiate outwardly what's truly within our authentic (albeit, often complex) selves. Our masks are jettisoned.

5

Notice

*Teens prefer the company of those their own
age more than ever before or after . . . merely
expressing in the social realm the teen's
general attraction to novelty and
excitement. . . . Teens gravitate toward peers
for another, more powerful reason: to invest in
the future rather than the past. We enter a
world made by our parents. But we will live
most of our lives, and prosper (or not) in a
world run and remade by our peers.*
—National Geographic

Erica, age 15, is a sharp, athletic, all-girls-private-high-school student with a sweet, pretty face and bright eyes. I wondered what pressures Erica encounters at school and from her parents to succeed and how she handles that stress. I was interested in knowing how her parents and family emotionally support her, and what her personal insights were as she navigates through not only high school, but also a stage of great personal change. I would discover that Erica has valuable advice for students and parents. She told me of high-school innovations, and that her parents "are there for me."

M: Thanks for sharing your thoughts. Do you think Chinese parents are overly stereotyped as super hard on their children, so that there is no room for less than A's?

E: I do. It's exaggerated. It's not true for most parents that nothing matters but excellent grades. My parents are human and flexible, but that said, my parents are also strict. Yes, it's about getting top grades, but also about being a well-rounded person. My mom pushes me to join clubs and volunteer, and I appreciate that she provides me with transportation. I'm in the High School Leadership Conference that includes students of all races. I like being part of a group that promotes and benefits from the diversity of cultures. My mom takes me to art classes. She also understands there are times when a fifteen-year-old needs to socialize with her friends. That's the flexible side of my mom. At the same time, I have demanding parents who expect A's, a high SAT, and meaningful extracurriculars such as volunteering. Luckily, even though I play team volleyball, I always finish my homework. We have "free" periods at school when I can do homework as well as time for study after dinner. I try to get to bed by 10:00 p.m. so I can wake up refreshed. A good night's sleep gives me the best feeling.

M: Glad you can sleep early and enjoy it. I found it interesting that the Dalai Lama once said sleep is the best meditation. Rest, revitalization, and recharging are needed to allow our brains to evolve optimally. On mini-surveys, many high-school students have ranked sleep as their favorite activity. Sleep is an issue for some of my students and sometimes causes heated arguments with parents. Staying up very late, students are often tired and sleep in class. I've encouraged students to nap before dinner, and for parents to let their children sleep in on weekends as much as possible; teens' bodies need sleep to accommodate rapid growth. Several students have told me they could tolerate late nights, as they could count on weekend rest. Many students support experimenting with a later starting time, and the use of Internet classes at home. Teens require 8–9 hours sleep, but average 7 to 7.5 (National Sleep Foundation, 2006); students are often overly stimulated by electronic devices right up to bedtime. There are occasions when teachers allow the student to put his or her head down and sleep.

E: A lot of students stay up late and have trouble rising in the morning. Parents and adolescents shouldn't fight about it if it can't be changed. Better support each other during high school, which is hard enough in itself. Parents should realize as long as their children are doing well that some will not be able to adjust to an early-to-bed, early-to-rise schedule. I also stay up until 1:00 a.m. for special projects or exam preparation.

M: Do you ever feel any pressure to use drugs? Isn't a lot of the drug use caused by peer pressure? I can still remember how much I wanted to be liked when I was in high school.

E: Definitely. As a 15-year-old, you might feel pressure to smoke marijuana to feel "in" or drink alcohol. I have a strong sense of my boundaries; I respect myself for not using drugs.

M: How young were you when you felt pressure to excel academically?

E: I wanted to be a ballerina from an early age, and didn't put so much attention on my studies. My parents told me how difficult it was to be a ballerina, and that I could suffer a possible injury. A ballerina goes through a great ordeal, and I had to face the fact that I wasn't motivated to endure it. By 8th grade, my parents told me to prepare for the private school entrance exam and to maintain all A's. At first I resisted my mom who insisted she knew what was right for me. It took a while before I understood the importance of preparing myself for an excellent high school. I began to study wholeheartedly. I have older brothers I call "burnt cookies." I learned from their mistakes and guidance to start early in high school to prepare for an outstanding university. I do feel pressure to be successful, so I have outlets such as sports, friends, and volunteering. My mom and I argue, but we work things out and I know she and my dad love me, even if we fight sometimes. We can't always agree. No child wants a parent to be angry at them; the child relies on the parent for just about everything, but we're moving to be more independent. (*Laughing*) Maybe one unnecessary pressure for me is to have a private piano teacher in high school. I've had a piano teacher since I was three. I enjoy playing but no longer feel the need for a piano teacher. It doesn't feel right if forced.

M: (*Laughing*) Glad you enjoy doing your own thing on the piano. You are appreciative and respectful toward your parents who encourage you to have a well-rounded education. At the same time, you are finding your own way. It's been illuminating talking with you. I'd like to ask one last question. Do you learn from your peers?

E: Definitely I learn a lot from my friends. It's important the friends you choose, super important. You learn because you can trust them. But that doesn't mean I don't learn from my parents and brothers as well.

****

Earl and his dad were on their way to lunch when Dad said they'd first do a short interview for this collaborative book. A hungry but willing Earl, a sophomore in high school, sat down with me and his dad to talk about "Tiger Moms." His dad is American, Mom from Taiwan. Apologizing that Mom is not present to give her opinion, Dad starts the interview.

D: Does your mom nag you at all to study?

E: Yes.

D: What's an example?

E: My mom tells me to read a book, even if I don't really need to study it. After I've finished studying a chapter, she will say review it. Our teacher wants us to

Notice

move at a pace he deems best. If I were to go back over material, it might hinder me from progressing.

D: So let's say you've done all the homework from the class and your mom wants you to study more, maybe go over the material again, go into it more deeply and get a leg up on your classmates. Why would that bother you?

E: It doesn't really annoy me because I know she's well intentioned. After many years of dealing with Mom, I know her patterns, and I don't react much.

D: You aren't ignoring your mother?

E: Of course not. I always take her opinion into consideration. Mom's right that review is good and, if I have time, I do it. It's just not helpful for me to always use my time to review. If there are more important and enjoyable things to do, then I will pursue them first.

D: How do you react to your mom asking you to do more homework when you have other things to do?

E: If Mom asks me to study more, I just say that I've done sufficient homework. I'm fine. It's when I've already done what was required, and Mom's nagging, then I might resist. Mom soon gives up and I emerge victorious.

M: What's the positive and negative in having a Tiger Mom?

E: I don't really think I have a Tiger Mom. I think she might qualify if my dad weren't such a Non-Tiger Dad. For me, it all evens out. Mom strongly pushes me to study more and Dad is like "whatever." So within this dynamic, I don't feel any strong impact of a Tiger Mom.

M: You still have the feeling your dad wants you to study seriously?

E: Yes, I do. He just has a different approach. Both my parents have the same goal for me, to study the best I can.

M: How do you stay tranquil when you are nagged? You mentioned you might have previously gotten angry, but that you now take it more in stride.

E: (*Laughing*) I stay calm, and Mom hates it. I become very logical. I present why my reasons are more acceptable than hers. It bugs her so much she again surrenders and walks away. What annoys her even more—and I think I'm a terrible person for doing it—if she uses a word in English incorrectly, I will correct her. Mom might use an improper tense, and I'll fix it for her. It really throws her off.

M: Have you reached the point in your high-school life where you find more self-motivation.

E: For some subjects, yes; others, no. I enjoy English so it's easier to do and also Chinese because the teacher really likes me, as I'm the only one in class with an American last name. I speak up quite a bit. One time I forgot my homework, and the teacher came up to me and said, "I'm sure you have a very legitimate excuse." In math, I'm not so motivated because I just don't enjoy it.

D: So you know you have to get excellent grades to get into a good college?

E: Yes, for sure.

D: So Mom urges you to do well in all your school subjects and especially in math and science? She is asking you to get A's in math and science when you are getting B's. She's worried that you won't get into a top university, and so is your father. Do you get extra help in those difficult classes?

E: I think Mom is really great when I ask for help. She doesn't nag me at all about it; she just gets me the help. The second I told her I needed tutoring in math and science, she started calling around until she found a tutor. Mom is very fair.

M: How do you cope with your need to sleep with the requirements of study? Some of the high-school students say they doze in class.

E: If I lose sleep during the week, I make it up on the weekend. If I had to, I could sleep during Speech class. We do a lot of concentrated work in Speech when a tournament is approaching, but otherwise the class is not demanding.

D: What time do you go to bed each school day?

E: At 11:30 and get up at 7:15.

M: What's the influence of your peer group and friends on your study activities?

E: My friends help me a lot. I eat with them, and sometimes ask about homework. I have my least favorite subjects, math and science, after lunch. One of my friends actually tutored me for a while during the lunch break.

****

Once, in the middle of a practice session,
she burst out,
"Stop it, Mommy. Just stop it."
"Lulu, I didn't say anything," I replied.
"I didn't say one word."
"Your brain is annoying me," Lulu said.
"I know what you're thinking."
—Amy Chua

Fifteen-year-old Brett is full of curiosity and ability, which are going to keep him at the top of his game in academics. He seldom misses the opportunity to ask questions, carefully learning and reviewing vocabulary, reading, grammar, and writing. He's a constant note-taker.

M: What's your opinion of the Tiger Mom? What's the positive and negative of Tiger Moms?

B: You're talking about strict Tiger Moms. They are logical and acceptable in our modern society, but in moderation. I would agree with Tiger Moms who insist that their children fulfill the obligation to study. I know how Tiger Moms feel, but they have to know when to be lenient as well. Tiger Moms who say no, absolutely no sleepovers, no choice for free time activities may be going too far. Moms who disproportionally nag to motivate may bring about the opposite effect. There's a picture of a parent standing over her child with a violin, saying "Until you get the piece right, you won't be given dinner." That's not reasonable. But some children need an extra push. Parents need to be involved without going to the extremes of hovering over the child's shoulder. That's usually too tense.

M: Don't you think that push helps you to study? Most high-school students I know need some urging to study, to keep up an acceptable effort?

B: I don't agree. There are certain students who do not need that push; they've been trained since they were little. They have the sense of self-discipline. I pride myself in studying well from my own inner motivation. Sometimes I fight with my mom because I feel my parents are taking that inner pride away from me by telling me something I already know. They're still treating me like a child—which is completely understandable—but sometimes parents have to be aware of what the student is going through, changing to be more than just a child. Parents need to see whether the child is capable of self-discipline. Depending on the child—everyone is different—the extra push of the Tiger Mom may be required. Tiger Moms have their rightful position. But parents have to be intelligent not just emotional. If the child can handle his or her homework and the results are fine, then leave him or her alone.

M: What's an example of having to practice self-discipline? You have a demanding high-school curriculum in honors classes.

B: There's a difference between responsibility and self-discipline. You have no option regarding responsibility, but you have a choice whether to practice some form of self-discipline. I mean the self-discipline that goes beyond your responsibility; it's your choice. It may affect you in a positive or negative way. But it's for you to choose. Studying the courses in my curriculum is not self-discipline in that I have no choice but to study. To do the work necessary to graduate with honors is not something I can say no to. It's like the responsibility of a job. After class, I can choose extracurricular activities, because they are what I want to do, not because I'm required to do them.

M: How do you get through those times when you feel resistive and just don't want to study?

B: That's when your sense of responsibility gets you through that barrier; you feel the tug of knowing you just have to do it. But when you don't have an inner sense of obligation, that's when the parents rightfully should push you, because you are being irresponsible.

M: Sometimes the parental push helps the student if it's called for?

B: Right. Let me tell you where self-discipline might go beyond the responsibility of the classroom. I like cross-country running, and I practice mile-runs within certain time parameters. This requires a sense of perseverance in an activity that I have no responsibility to take part in. When you're running long distances your legs get so tired, your brain gives out. What keeps you going is your heart, the passion to do it. So while your legs are telling you to stop, your heart actually tells your brain, hey, if you want to accomplish some good, be the best you can, you need self-discipline. You have to discipline your legs and run the mile.

M: Students sleep during some school classes; they study until 2:00 a.m. to read the textbook, finish homework, and prepare for tests. More are using the Internet for information, blogging, posting, and receiving assignments. As long as they do well on their tests, some students don't worry about paying attention in class, using it to make up for lost sleep. The teacher sometimes leaves the student alone. It's unfortunate that class time, school facilities, a decent teacher, are all being wasted. A shut-down brain is a missed opportunity; shouldn't you be learning, and perhaps in a free period, practicing, doing homework? I understand the student still gets top grades, but is the student using the most efficient time-management? How do you manage your study schedule and need for sleep? Is there any time to take a nap?

B: I'm not the person to ask about this. I am just the person you described, staying up until 2:00 a.m. I don't intentionally do it, but I sometimes nod off in class. I doze off, but I catch myself before actually going to sleep. I can't help it. My eyes get heavy; sometimes I feel exhausted from staying up late and getting up early.

M: I think in that case, not as a common occurrence, the attentive teacher would most likely let the student doze.

B: Yes, they usually do.

M: If I have a student who occasionally puts his or her head down and sleeps a short while, I just let it go. But more than that, I think it's important to find out why the student has to sleep in class.

B: My New Year's resolution for 2012 is to arrange my study schedule, to organize myself by paying attention to time, a filing system, and convenient environment. I'm taking it step by step, and slowly I'm managing to get to sleep earlier. But you have to understand the competition in high school today if you choose to go for one of the best universities. You actually have to stay up until 2:00 a.m. sometimes.

M: So don't you think it's a good idea to have a conversation with your family and yourself about sleep, as with food, exercise, hard work, breaks, being healthy?

B: Definitely, it's about balance. That's what my New Year's resolution is about. I'm considering going to bed early and getting up early to do my homework.

M: Do you have any advice for high-school students who argue with their parents about homework?

B: If they have a way to resolve difficulties, they don't need to fight. It's a matter of going to extremes. Occasionally fights will happen, but they don't need to drag on. I wouldn't give advice, because everyone is different. It would be wrong to give a general guideline that applies to all. Each child and parent is unique. You can't expect everyone to fall within a general norm. People have their characteristics and personalities. The parent has to understand what the daughter or son is like, and if he or she is not fulfilling his or her academic responsibility. If children are not performing, Tiger Moms have the right to push them to complete their assignments. Of course, no parent has the right to go so far as to physically or emotionally abuse his or her child, which is an extreme. In fact, I would like to change the word "push" to "guide" children to study, to create a very conducive environment for learning that removes the feeling of being forced. The environment, including sometimes necessary parental urging, should be felt as supportive, propelling the student in a more natural way, than, for example, excessive yelling. Psychologically, the student feels comfortable or uncomfortable according to the environment.

M: Well said, thanks. Do you feel a lot of pressure to excel academically?

B: Yes, most of my classmates do.

M: How young were you when you first realized, wow, I've got to do this. I have to tackle the world of study in a serious, intelligent way? And it's going to be hard sometimes, but I'm determined to keep going.

B: Starting in second grade, I received B's and C's. After arguing with the teacher, I received detention. I yelled at her violently. Later I thought she was cool when she said she was wrong and apologized, while saying at the same time I was also wrong to raise my voice. I likewise apologized. It wasn't until the seventh grade that my environment and my psychological state changed. I had friends, classmates who excelled in all their studies. That good company taught me to strive, to go out and do my best. My peer group set such a positive example for me. It was very strong. Seventh grade was my period of enlightenment. I started doing my best and excelling. I actually put in the effort. Without my friends, I don't know where I'd be today. Before seventh grade I was a loner. I didn't have a friend, no one to actually relate to. In seventh grade, I found three people who changed my daily monotony with the fun of friendship. Before I had no conscious goal, nothing exciting that I wanted to achieve. No one motivated me until I fell in with this group of friends. They changed the way I looked at myself. It was a new world. I started to work much harder but also enjoyed life with my friends. My perspective seemed to be changing every day.

I've since moved on. I don't need to be motivated as much by the example of my peers; I'm doing my work more on my own, more self-inspired. It's much easier once you've been inspired by others to become self-motivated. It's great if students are self-motivated but not to the extent that all outer motivation, such as from teachers and parents, is ignored. Now, I want a passionate, intimate relationship in my life, but it was the experience of actually being liked and welcomed by these friends that put me on the right path.

M: Would you like to ask yourself any question?

B: What do I want to do? What's my heart's desire? There are two paths in front of me: I could live each day in the moment—carefree, happy, and relaxed or I could sacrifice immediate satisfaction for a goal of success in the future. I may not always be happy now, but in the future I might find a satisfying happiness. Currently, I'm debating whether to find happiness now, go with the flow, see what happens, try my best without going overboard, do what I want, go for it, or keep preparing diligently for tomorrow, a path which doesn't give me much immediate happiness.

M: To use your word, could there be a "balance"? Does a life of study have to be only drudgery?

B: It's not that I don't want balance, but I don't find a middle road. I'm looking for it. Now I'm mostly going in the direction of being the best student I can be. I don't have it yet, but I agree with you. I want to achieve my goals and be happy at the same time. What better way to live my life?

M: Thanks so much. That's a spectacular addition to our conversation.

****

Bamboo Bending

As somebody who's visited a lot of schools, you can tell very quickly when you go into a school whether there's a patina of respect, whether there's genuine respect or whether there's just disrespect. And it's very hard to do any kind of learning in a disrespectful atmosphere.
—Howard Gardner

Tiffany is a tall, bright sophomore, energetic and thoughtful. Born in China, she came to the USA when she was ten years old.

M: Is your mom a Tiger Mom? Is she strict?

T: My mom is not strict. She always tells me to stop studying at night and go to sleep, but doesn't try to force me anymore. My mom doesn't even necessarily check my grades. She says it's my responsibility. I like that she gives me my space.

M: Do you feel pressure to succeed in school?

T: I put a lot on myself, but not from my parents, no. I'm programmed, even before the influence of my parents, to try my best. If I don't study well, I won't have a job. When my mom tries to put any pressure on me, I can be mean to her. I like my dad because he's never demanding.

M: You already think about having a job?

T: Yes. I hope I can hone my abilities. I like when the teachers talk about skills, which might later lead to a job. High school is the most important time for me, because it will get me into a university. High school has pressure, but in university I believe I will be more settled; I will concentrate on preparing for a career. I started in eighth grade to be serious about school and to achieve good grades.

M: What subjects are the most interesting to you?

T: None. I don't care for class. I do my best. I've learned to concentrate even if I'm bored. I pay attention in class so I don't have to waste time at home learning the material. I just self-talk myself into concentrating.

M: Do you take notes in class?

T: Depends. Usually only if it's required, but I want to try to use note taking as active learning, to keep my mind running.

M: How do you handle homework? What's your environment and schedule like?

T: I get home, and I might play on the computer (watching TV shows) for two hours to relax. Then I will study from about nine to twelve with some breaks for a snack or a short walk. I could be more organized; my study area is messy.

M: You have the Internet available to assist with your study?

T: Yes, but it can be a big temptation just to use the computer for fun. I try not to use the Internet too much, because I know I'll end up playing. The Internet is great for learning, but I can't always control myself. Sometimes I put off my homework, but later have regrets because eventually the teacher wants it. Usually the homework isn't as bad as I imagine. I do use YouTube to help me understand the textbook and google when I don't know what something means.

M: Do you volunteer?

T: I do. University admissions committees want to see volunteer service, but I actually like it. I learn about how the greater society works, how communities have to pull together to complete projects. I have a good feeling when I've contributed my energy. That's social intelligence, right? We are separate human beings and also interconnected. We need to help each other, because there are times for all of us when we're down.

M: You study art?

T: Unlike my academics, art is fun for me. I like what I draw, and I've started a portfolio, which will help me get into a good university. When I was a young girl in China, my parents forced me to take art, dance, and piano. It was too much, and my parents let me drop the classes. I have studied art in the United States since I was ten years old. I love it. It's beautiful to express feelings inside me in a painting or a drawing. Chinese schools need to let children be more free to perform arts; American schools need more determined, diligent and self-directed students.

M: In our times when technology quickly becomes obsolete, Daniel Pink has made a strong case for arts education belonging in students' core curriculum along with science, technology, engineering, mathematics, and literature. You're exposed to the creative process of art, and you light up when you talk about it. Art gives you a lot of satisfaction. What do you do in your leisure time?

T: Shopping with friends at the mall. I like action movies, magazines, and books that tell very intriguing, personal stories. I don't read as much as I'd like; I enjoyed the *Twilight* series when I was younger. Nothing beats going to a Korean pop concert where a gorgeous guy is singing great and dancing like crazy.

M: You have good friends?

T: My peers are absolutely important to me. At school my classmates are mostly friendly. But I don't think any guy's going to ask me out because I'm too tall. Anyway, most Asian parents think high-school boys are not mature enough to date. Girls develop faster; some high-school girls have boyfriends in college. My mom wouldn't care if I went out with a boy, but she would want to see him before we left on our first date. I know one girl who has dated fourteen guys already as a sophomore. Even in 8th grade, some girls start dating. But so far, not me.

M: What advice do you give students who are new immigrants from China? Some students complain their parents nag them, and treat them as if they were in China.

T: I'd ask the student if he or she were really putting in an effort to do his/her best. Usually high-school students in the USA, like me, want to avoid hard work, whereas kids in China are more used to it. Chinese kids in general are more eager to please their parents. I'd say, "Are you sure you are giving enough time and energy to schoolwork, so that your parents won't nag?" If you are not, you are the one who has to change.

When I apply myself, I gain valuable knowledge and habits. I would never do homework if I weren't motivated. It's not the subject matter which motivates me, but the goal of attending a university. It doesn't matter if I'm bored and have to force myself to study. So I'd say, first of all, make sure you study on a steady basis. A parent from China most likely will nag if you are lazy about homework. If you are doing your best, and the nagging continues, it's your parent who needs to change. Be sure you find ways to recreate and refresh yourself.

M: What skills do you want from high school beyond just passing tests and getting your diploma with a decent GPA? What would prepare you for our rapidly changing times? What abilities and academic habits do you want to take with you to the university and into the world, which you and your peers will soon be running?

T. (*Laughing*) Yeah! No more studying dull subjects after high school. (*Laughing*) I think an absolutely necessary skill is how to relate to various kinds of people of diverse races and different sexual orientations. It's hard sometimes to get along, but it's always been rewarding for me to appreciate someone who is a nonconventional yet genuine person. I think teachers should educate us to respect people, just as we want to be respected. There's lots of diversity, and we should make the most of it, rather than separate people on the basis of different cultures, religions, and sexual preferences. I don't like kissing up to people in the "in crowd." Why would you want to make yourself what you are not in order to be accepted? We need to respect all, not just certain "in" people. Can the teachers impart that basic teaching? How can we succeed in this big, wide world in peace without accepting everyone for who they are?

M: Well said, Tiffany. You say, "No more studying," after high school, and I can feel your excitement and also that you're kidding. You're really saying no more boring studying? You know now that study will be ongoing as you begin your career? The world is changing so fast, even after university, you may continue to study and attend seminars, lectures, and symposiums as you develop your career. You'll find interests extending beyond work. You may be surprised to hear that in ancient Greece, one of the celebrated statesmen and sages, Solon, said: "I will happily grow old learning new things."

T: (*Laughing*) Maybe, but don't count on it. I just want to get through high school. That was fun talking with you.

****

Jacob's Taiwanese mom was born in Vietnam; his dad, also Taiwanese, was born in Taiwan. Jacob is 13 years old, born in the United States.

M: What do you think about Tiger Moms? Do you think that Asian parents are overly stereotyped as being unreasonably strict?

J: Yes, they are overly stereotyped. The majority of Asian parents are not necessarily insistent that their children only become doctors, lawyers and high-paying professionals. Usually though, parents want their children to work hard; they are more open-minded than given credit for.

M: How long have you been motivated to do well in school? Since what age did you decide to become an outstanding student?

J: When I was only seven years old, our school had a career day. Kids were asked to come to school dressed as they imagined themselves as working adults. They gave us fliers for our parents to help us prepare. My dad asked me what I wanted to be, and I said I wanted to be an MD, which is still my aspiration.

M: How do you handle homework?

J: Usually when I get home, I'll start the easier, shorter homework. I'll do the tougher subjects after dinner. Most of the time during the week, I limit my video games or watching TV. My parents might ask me about my homework, if I'm playing games or watching TV too much.

M: Do you feel a tension between studying versus playing an exciting game or watching a show. Is there a small struggle you have to work out for yourself?

J: Yes, sometimes it's like that.

M: Do you feel pressure to achieve straight As? Do you feel it's a burden? Or is your dedication to study something you pursue happily?

J: I don't feel like it's overly burdensome. For some reason, I have to try to get a bad grade.

M: You would have to try to get a lower grade when you take your tests? I used to hate guys like you.

J: (*Both laughing*) I need to be having an extremely bad day to even have the chance to get less than an A.

M: You have to try to get a bad grade, because you are already prepared when you are taking the test. It's not difficult for you, because you've done the work to master the material?

J: Exactly. I really have to be off my game to do poorly.

M: Your environment for your work is comfortable and organized, with a good file system, Internet connected?

J: Yes.

M: Even when you're studying hard, you take short breaks?

J: Yes, sometimes breaks that are too long. But I need them. I get a snack.

M: Do you have choices in your extracurriculars, or do your parents tell you what to do after school?

J: My parents had me take piano lessons, but I didn't like the idea, especially at first. I felt forced.

M: How old were you?

J: I was seven years old when I started piano.

M: What was your musical learning journey like?

J: I still take piano. One of my teachers was a director of an orchestra. She was very strict. My mom wanted me to have this chance. She was so tough, Chinese, and charged $50 an hour. My mom was sure I'd practice at least an hour every day, sometimes more of course. I got burnt out; it was too much. I lost interest, so I quit for a while.

Later I said, OK, I have to take violin. It was one of those ten-minute deals; I just knew I wanted to try a new instrument. That was an enjoyable experience with a nice violin teacher, an elderly Chinese man. When he retired, I also quit violin for a while, but it was a great learning time for me. I saw how a teacher can be enjoyable and at the same time demanding.

I found another American violin teacher who was well into his seventies, tired and lacking the energy to be a good teacher. He couldn't hear well. If I played the wrong note, he was unable to correct me, so I started to lose my ability to play the violin. At this time, my mom arranged for me to take piano classes with a German teacher; he's a college student, about 23 years old. He's an excellent teacher; I'm happy.

M: Researchers have said even two or three years of music training heightens auditory perception and sharpens focusing, short-term memory, organizing, and reasoning. Do you feel your music study helps you in your other studies?

J: A lot. I'm not a good artist at all but I have some real musical talent. It's actually both fun and demanding to develop that talent. I haven't yet developed an ear to listen to music deeply, but I find that playing music matters to me very much. I love instruments such as the saxophone for the school band. I still find the violin enjoyable to play, though I'm not excellent at it. I continue to benefit and learn more about piano.

M: What's more difficult to play?

J: For me piano, because you have to train the two hands to do different actions. It's hard to coordinate them.

M: How do you handle nagging from Mom for you to study more? Do you ever yell back?

J: Anyone will lose his or her temper at some point. I do. I usually handle it by going to my room and sleeping. Anger and yelling take away all my energy. I have a nap and then I'm fine.

M: Glad you can admit it. In many of our discussions about Tiger Moms, we sometimes neglect to mention Tiger Kids who can be as ballistic as moms and dads. (*Both laughing*)

You always have a chance to reconnect with your mom?

J: Sure. Everything's OK with some time and space. So that's a good thing about my mom.

M: Yes, that's great you have a way to reconcile and return to the more normal peaceful household, right? You don't let things build up.

J: It helps me to be alone sometimes and sleep or lie down and relax myself. I am also learning to let my mom do the same.

M: Can you talk about matters with your best friends that you'd be reluctant to talk about with your parents?

J: For sure.

M: Yet is your family still the most important to you?

J: Yes, but my peers are extremely important. But family is first. At the same time, friends are a part of a good life.

M: What motivates you to study, to practice piano? You can get by with minimal study, but you always study two to three hours every night, sometimes more. You express the desire to understand what you are doing, whether it is learning to write or playing piano.

J: I really want to learn. You are always emphasizing practice, whether it is grammar or piano. There is so much out there to learn. I want to understand; that's why I study.

M: You're a teacher's dream.

J: (*Laughing*) I like that. When I start high school next year, I'll get even more serious. My main goal in high school is to have a 4.0 GPA and maybe even be valedictorian. I have high expectations for myself.

M: You want to be a medical doctor? You're gaining skills that will match your high expectations for yourself, yes?

J: Right. Yes, that's what I want, and I know I have to study to be able to accomplish that goal to become a doctor as well as a learned and well-rounded person.

My parents and teachers advise me to keep growing intellectually, emotionally, and spiritually. I'm just becoming more aware of these aspects of my personality.

M: Do you have any advice for other students who complain about their moms and dads yelling excessively about study?

J: I would listen to Mom. At the same time, don't totally pay attention to her screaming at you. Ignore some aspect of it, but still get what she is trying to communicate to you. Block out the insulting parts of what she's saying, but understand that maybe you should study more. You have to keep your cool to assess the true situation. Most moms and dads want their children to study, and what's wrong with that? But how moms/dads and sons relate emotionally is important, as I'm learning.

M: A student tells you: "I'm having such a hard time to make my homework interesting. I'm so bored with my high school. The study seems so unimportant to me."

J: You have to think of ways to make study fun. Think of it as an elaborate game. For example, studying and actually taking a test. Imagine a challenge to get the best grade possible. If I received an 88 last test, can I score a 95? That's something to strive for. Even 100% can come into your imagination. Regarding homework, break the materials into small parts to better understand. Really catch the meaning before going on. Also take short breaks from thinking and concentrating. Relax, get a snack, watch some TV, but go back to study until you are satisfied that you have done a decent job. You might even take a nap before or after dinner. I do. I've taken showers to relax my body when staying up late to finish a project.

****

Bamboo Bending

Let me tell you about a place out east
Just 15 minutes from the L.A. streets
Hollywood doesn't even know we exist
Like it's a mystical land
Filled with immigrants . . . .
Six-two-six, young, wild and free.
(YouTube rap on 626, area code of
much of the San Gabriel Valley)
—David & Andrew Fung

Gerald, a high-school junior, is seventeen years old, born to Chinese parents in the United States; he lived in China for 10 years. His dad remains in Nanjing, China, while Gerald lives with his mom who plans to reunite with her husband in China. Gerald is a pleasant, intelligent, soulful student who asks wonderful questions and pays attention during an entire class, with breaks and some conversation of course. I'm grateful for such students.

M: Do you feel Tiger Moms and Dads are overly stereotyped as inflexible, strict and demanding parents when it comes to study? The other day I overheard a Latino student say to a Chinese student: "I feel so sorry for you that you have such strong parents when it comes to study; you're pushed a lot. You're going to be screamed at all the time. Don't feel too bad, there are some Mexican Tiger Moms as well."

G: For the most part, the stereotype is true in my case. I am pushed quite a bit. I have little choice but to excel. Actually my dad is somewhat open, but both parents are strict.

M: So you feel pressured to perform well in school?

G: Sometimes quite a bit, but now I can handle it.

M: You take good care of your health?

G: Yes, I'm better at it. And, you know, not all Asian parents are Tigers all the time. My parents are concerned for my well-being. Sometimes I can't meet their expectations, but they are accepting and loving of me regardless.

M: What's your motivation to apply yourself to study?

G: In the beginning, it was just because of my parents. Later I began to get used to a life of mostly study.

M: What subjects do you like the best?

G: Not one. I don't like any particular subject in high school; in middle school, I liked only biology.

M: Do you get any sense of satisfaction when you study and master some material? Do you find you are learning to think? Do you rest and relax?

G: Yes, I'm learning to master my high-school subjects. Last year, I spent two months studying chemistry non-stop with a tutor. I had to complete four thick packets of chemistry exercises. Later I received a 4 on my AP Chemistry exam. I was happy. The highest score is a 5. To celebrate and recuperate, I spent a weekend of fun, sleep and relaxation.

M: That accomplishment made you feel good.

G: Yes, it sure did. This feeling is also a motivation for studying my best for the SAT exam.

M: If you finish your homework in an hour, do you use some time to read, listen to YouTube lectures, view educational films, study for SAT?

G: I do have that plan, especially to study for AP tests, but I don't always follow through. I spent extra time studying for the SAT. The study paid off, because I knew what the exercises would be, and I had plenty of practice to apply to each kind of question.

M: When you are on Facebook, and you know you have to study, how do you discipline yourself to stop and redirect your attention?

G: It's very hard. It's a willful effort, placing myself in an environment away from temptation. I seldom study in my bedroom, because I have my computer there. I use the dining room or my mom's room. I make it so I won't have any distractions. I program myself you might say.

M: Are you sometimes immersed in cyberspace and Mom walks in and yells at you to get to work? How do you and Mom relate about homework?

G: (*Laughing*) There are times when my mom nags me for an extended period of time. I cannot say a word. I stay quiet and take it. I did at one time yell back, but it made the situation worse. So I don't do anything. I don't want to argue with my mom. She might even ground me, which is the worst thing for me. I want to be with my friends, not just at home. Sometimes I say, "Mom, I'm going to start my work now, really." Also I know moms can get angry when you might not expect it or understand why. That's just Mom.

M: And you also think, yes, I should be studying now?

G: That's right. I know my mom worries about my future.

M: Do you use the Internet for study?

G: Sometimes sure. If I want to study though, knowing myself, I have to turn off the computer.

M: Learning to concentrate, even when stressed, is part of your training?

G: Yes, that's a skill I'll need when I go to work. I had such a hard time concentrating for calculus finals. It was difficult material so the night before the final at 11:00 p.m., I was still sitting in front of these incomprehensible pages. Then, from somewhere I just got started and was able to concentrate by breaking the work into small pieces. I stayed up very late that night.

M: When you do study for longer periods do you give yourself breaks?

G: I do. If I'm very tired, I will go to bed earlier, wake up early and finish my homework. Actually it's better sometimes because my brain is fresh after sleep. I get up at 6:00 a.m. or so.

M: What advice do you give your friends who might be having a difficult relationship with a parent about school?

G: You have to compromise with your parents. Of course, you can't just do as you please, but the parent has to listen to you and you to the parent. You have to be willing to ask for the help of a tutor if necessary and your parents can afford it. You have to work at least a reasonable amount. (*Laughing*) There's no escape. That's what you and my friends also tell me.

****

Calvin Loo was born in China; he came to Los Angeles when he was ten years old. He's reflective about his high-school studies, and experiments with different ways of learning.

M: How do you view study? How do you best learn?

C: Learning is the way you can understand and comprehend what was previously unknown and mysterious. If, for example, you read the math book and answer the questions, that's study. It's better not to worry about the tests. Understand the problems and challenge yourself to solve them. Use the Internet to see sample problems and solutions. If you don't figure out how to do the problems, ask for help. Once you catch it, you'll do fine on the tests. My sisters tutored me in English because my parents did not speak English fluently.

M: You learn about science, math, history, and literature. Are there other skills you can learn to help you in your life and later in the workplace? Do you feel too young to have that concern?

C: My parents have taken me to their work. I will soon have to enter the world beyond school. I am picking up some practical skills in elective courses such as typing, MS Office, and woodshop. Our school teaches basic technology and how to use knowledge to solve specific problems, which we will be doing in our adult lives. I like to listen to people in the community who talk about different trades and professions. It's not too early to explore possible future occupations, and to learn corresponding skills.

M: Do you learn in group activities?

C: It works most of the time to solve problems as a group. We have to learn how to work together for a common goal. In the future, I may be doing a work project with my colleagues—some of whom maybe I won't like—but I need that ability to solve a problem in collaboration. I'm getting better at navigating the social aspects of school. I hope my IQ and EQ will both be high.

M: How do you handle working with a classmate you do not like?

C: I pretend I'm fine with him; I concentrate on the work. I don't take things too personally unless I'm adversely affected.

M: How would you describe the art of thinking something through?

C: It's very important as it relates to the wise and unwise choices we make. We need to discriminate what is or is not to our advantage, imagining different scenarios and consequences. We take information in, weigh and compare it, and then decide courses of action.

Notice

M: You wanted to ask me three questions?

C: Are you genuinely concerned with your job as a teacher, which affects people and society into the future? If I didn't have my teachers, I would be different than I am today. They have changed me mostly for the good. Are you worried about your profession wherein teachers are criticized for doing a poor job of educating? Knowing that children are depending on you, do you do your job in a competent and caring manner, while making the best of new technology?

M: Those are important questions. I'm concerned with the low ranking of American education. Parents, teachers and students must continue to reform. Students must step up and be part of the efforts to invigorate high-school education.

I try to affect my students in a positive way, relating to the way each learns as an individual. I encourage the interconnectivity of all schools in order to access the best technology and educational materials, and to continue flexible scheduling. Already colleges and high schools have courses online. California State University is responding to Governor Jerry Brown's mandate to utilize online learning and new technologies by establishing Web-based science labs and online courses. Through webcam monitors, proctors oversee tests for the growing number of credit courses on the Internet. This is not to supplant the classroom, but to complement it by adding more choices for the student and the teacher. What works at one high school or college might not be useful at another.

C: Do you prefer teaching at a private or public school, and which do you consider better?

M: I enjoy teaching both. Teaching is a science-based art and a great privilege. As you say, the teacher affects the students' growth. I tell my students that they too are the teacher.

C: I agree with that. The individual has to absorb and organize what is learned, adapt, and choose what works. Do you think teens are overly absorbed in computers and video games?

M: It's very addicting to have immediate excitement and feedback from a game or Facebook. One of the skills we need is the ability to focus, to be able to let go of a game or stop texting. American workers face the same challenge. Use the Internet not just for fun, but for its ability to help your studies.

C: That makes sense. You're saying we have to think about goals, not just keep ourselves constantly entertained.

6

Inter-Connect

*By working well, I mean when high
expectations are complemented with love,
understanding and parental involvement. . . .
But I also know of people raised with "tough
love" who are not happy and who resent their
parents. There is no easy formula for
parenting, no right approach (I don't believe,
by the way, that Chinese parenting is
superior). The best rule of thumb I can think of
is that love, compassion, and knowing your
child have to come first whatever culture
you're from.*
—Amy Chua

*Studies show that when parents engage and
guide their teens with a light but steady hand
staying connected but allowing independence,
their kids generally do much better in life.
Adolescents want to learn primarily, but not
entirely, from their friends.*
—National Geographic

A student's father dropped by early before class to
speak about his daughter, a high-school junior,
who, to the consternation of her family, could not
seem to get straight A's. Coming to the United States at
age 11, she struggled with English. She found herself
constantly arguing with her parents about not achieving
the grade point average necessary to get into a top
university. She had private tutoring, but could not get
past B's except for Physical Education and Art. Dad
was concerned as his daughter was held to an
extremely high family expectation, and thought she
was daydreaming and not willing to make the effort to

"get over the hump." He would start off civilly talking with his daughter and then get heated about how she was letting him down. He'd later feel terrible, because he truly cared and wanted the best for her. He intimated he was beginning to doubt himself and the family's insistence on a 4.0 grade average. It frightened him when the girl would respond with self-denigrating remarks, cry, go to her room and slam the door.

Dad said his daughter was an outstanding artist, and that she had won awards, seemed to love it, but the family, though appreciative of her talent, was focused on academics. When he asked for my opinion, I could only say what he most likely already knew, that young people don't all fit into the same mold, but have different abilities and ways to learn. Dad talked a while about his Asian education. In his family, if you studied enough, you would get excellent grades. He said he knew young people had different inclinations and abilities, but worried that a lack of academic perfection could result in missing out on a great university and a high-paying professional career. Unreasonable expectations led to disharmony between the father and daughter. I thought it was promising that Dad was facing and wanting to resolve the problem. After all, the daughter still had a bright future even if she did not go to a renowned university. He had already made up his mind to make peace with his daughter and compromise, but had to formulate a strategy that would make both the daughter and the family happy.

I asked Dad if he liked his daughter's art. Softening, he told me how proud he was when his daughter received an art award. "She paints beautifully and her art inspires unexpected emotions. I'm culturally ingrained to tell my daughter to put in extra hours to get an A. I understand that doesn't work for everyone, and shouldn't make us less proud of our children. She doesn't feel as appreciated for her accomplishments as she should. I want her to feel proud of herself."

In the movie, *Moneyball*, Peter Brand is the assistant general manager and statistics genius of the Oakland Athletics, and wants to show the general manager, Billy Beane (Brad Pitt) a video. Beane is dejected because the Athletics have just lost in the postseason. It's a video about a player who hits a homerun—his first ever in many at bats. Head down, and not realizing the ball has sailed over the fence, he overruns first base and slides back into first. Everyone's cheering and yelling at the player: "You hit a homer, get up, run the bases." Finally the embarrassed player gets up and rounds the bases to the cheers of the fans. The player never thought he could hit a home run, even after slamming one. Beane had just assembled a team—with a limited budget— that not only made it to the post season but set the American League record of winning twenty straight games, an amazing accomplishment. Peter Brand wanted Beane to see that even if the team wasn't number one, he should nonetheless enjoy the "home runs" he hit in a very exciting season.

****

It's one thing to say we are wasting kids' time and straining parent-kid relationships, but what's unforgivable is if homework is damaging our kids' interest in learning, undermining their curiosity.
—Alfie Kohn, author

Parent: I came home late and checked on my son, a high-school sophomore. He was intently playing video games. He said he finished all his homework. I couldn't believe he had so little homework, and even if he finished, why wasn't he still studying? What about reviewing? SAT? Writing practice? I think high-school students, as a general rule, should study a minimum of three hours an evening. For me, learning is exciting, even if sometimes laborious. I want my son to take study seriously and also experience the interesting, satisfying moments of understanding a topic. Today, in so many fields, the worker is asked to comprehend quickly changing material—really get it—and adapt that knowledge to the task at hand. My son needs to learn to think flexibly. I hate to see the homework time wasted. What's your opinion about homework?

M: Some teenagers want to escape study, or get by with the least amount of work. They feel homework is boring compared to exciting social interacting or video games. Teachers have to make homework more challenging and interesting, so students can practice important skills, such as analyzing, global thinking, comparing and contrasting, evaluating, adapting knowledge to new situations, and utilizing resources such as the media. I ask the class to share the responsibility for creating interest in the homework. While acknowledging how important a healthy emotional and social life is, I agree that the students should devote consistently two to three hours an evening to study, with breaks, sometimes studying less, and other times more. Duke University's Harris Cooper, after analyzing dozens of studies, concluded middle and high-school students who do homework score better on standardized tests, but doing more than 60 to 90 minutes a night in middle school and more than two hours in high school resulted in lower scores. The quality of study time has to be considered carefully, as well as the capacity of the individual student. Teenagers in Japan, Denmark and the Czech Republic have less assigned homework, but are scoring higher than their American counterparts. Some countries such as Iran, Greece, and Thailand give loads of homework, but the students do poorly in standardized tests. Social conditions must be taken into account. No matter how much homework a student is given, if he's dodging bullets, suffering from political/economic collapse, and widespread poverty, how will he have great success with testing? Preparing for tests isn't the only purpose of homework; Harris Cooper supports homework as it develops study habits, time-management skills, and self-discipline. Self-discipline is the ability to direct one's attention, utilizing emotional and cognitive resources, to the task at hand in order to achieve one's goals. Certainly parents can over-schedule their children. Reviewing the book, *The Over-Scheduled Child, Avoiding the Hyper-Parenting Trap* by Dr. Alvin Rosenfeld and Nicole Wise, Dr. David Spiegel comments: "The authors expertly dissect our contemporary preoccupation with power parenting. They show us what is wrong with the 'isms': consumerism, perfectionism, protectionism. Our success as a technological and commercial culture has led us astray—we no longer trust our instincts, emotions, and relationships. We feel we have to plan, organize, and purchase the successful development of our children rather than enjoy its unfolding. In our desire to provide the best for our children we manage rather than love them."

****

To be yourself in a world that is constantly trying to make you something else is the greatest accomplishment.
—Ralph Waldo Emerson

I spoke with Anna, who related her experience with her high-school son. Both she and her son were born in Taiwan.

M: Were you a Tiger Mom?

A: I was a Tiger Mom and Tiger Dad. I divorced when my son was six years old. Raising him by myself, I carried both parental responsibilities. I had a future picture of my son, which filled me with excitement and high expectation.

M: Did you notice a change in your son when he began high school?

A: My son and I were good friends when he was little. We played in the park, enjoyed food in restaurants, and went to the zoo to see different animals. We had a very good time. I truly appreciated his company. Things changed when he was a teenager. He made friends from school, and would talk to his friends instead of me.

M: How about school?

A: He didn't study, and his report cards were terrible. We had so many long talks about it. I scolded him to think about his future. He promised he would study harder. But the report cards appeared with the same C's. Again I would become upset. I felt helpless. I sought advice from other parents and took him to see a specialist; I used rewards, and I hired a tutor to teach him after school, even though we didn't have much money. I gave my best effort, but he didn't improve (failing time and time again). I was so tired and frustrated that I yelled at him, losing my temper. Our relationship was tense, and we had some terrible arguments. What could I do to make him change? I could not let him down. Why wasn't he preparing to go to a university? What could I do for him? I felt so upset. I cried myself to sleep many nights. God help me, I prayed.

M: Did you come to some resolution? Were you able to have a serious and meaningful talk with your son? Did any particular event cause you to rethink your attitude about your son and study?

A: One day after dinner, I talked about his cousins. They were all straight "A" students. My son became nervous, frozen in his body, sitting there with his head bent. He didn't utter a word, but I kept saying, "I wish one day I could be proud of my son." Shocking me, he started to cry. He had never cried before, even when his father disappeared from his life. I didn't know what to do. I wanted to hug him but I didn't. The air was tense and uncomfortable. When we went home that night, I knew I had to make sure I was acting in his best interests.

M: Did your son start to study more seriously after that?

A: He would sit down and study but soon would fall sleep. The study could not capture his interest. I shook my head. What's wrong with him? Why can't he just concentrate? Is he my sweet little boy who wanted to please his mother? I saw his innocent face, sound asleep. Suddenly, a bell of recognition rang in my brain, "What is my foremost concern? Happy, I wish him to be happy. That's right, isn't it? Yes, that is what I most care about. Look now, is he happy?"

M: So you changed your way of thinking?

A: Maybe I was wrong. I had put him in a mold of my own making. Unlike academic studies, he was proficient at and enjoyed repairing electronic and electrical items. The lion in the movie *Born Free* isn't happy until he's back where he belongs. Perhaps I was forcing my son to be in the academic world that was not natural for him.

M: You became open to the idea that your son's success wasn't limited to being an A student in high school?

A: I realized I didn't need to only focus on schoolwork. The world is large and full of possibilities. We don't need to lock ourselves in our habitual expectation, ignoring the child in front of us. So I made a very important decision: "I set you free." It doesn't mean I gave up on him. I still asked him to study, but not with the same insistence, and with a new idea that my son's future would be in mastering a practical art, rather than an academic one. I stopped yelling at him.

M: How did your relationship change?

A: We had a much better relationship, becoming good friends again. We started talking and laughing, and I continued to encourage him. If I couldn't change him, then I would change myself. Finally, he graduated from high school, and he didn't continue on to college.

M: So what did you and your son plan?

A: I let him understand that since he chose not to go school, he had to work. He had abilities that would make him valuable to a good company. His cousins all went to excellent universities. My co-workers and my classmates bragged about how great these universities were. I listened and was happy for them. But it didn't affect how I felt about my son. I no longer compared my son to other children. I told myself: every kid is different. I was happy for the change I made.

M: So how's your son doing?

A: My son is 26 years old, and is an engineer in a big company. By discovering his talent and then excelling at it, he earns $100,000 a year. Without taking university engineering courses, he acquired hands-on knowledge. The company saw potential in my son and trained him in the use of high-tech equipment. He enjoys exploring state-of-the-art technology. When he started as an assistant engineer, he was only eighteen years old. He knew he didn't have a degree, so he was willing to take any opening position. Full of energy, because he was doing what he was capable of doing, his eyes would shine when talking about his work. He is changed; he looks like a new person. His boss promoted him, and he learned to use more sophisticated machinery. He was happy and confident. He found his value from a satisfying career. Now he takes a college course in his free time. That is his choice, not my pushing. I feel relaxed now. At my last birthday get together, he asked me "Mom, are you proud of me?"

"Yes. . . . " I laughed, and this time I cried and gave him a warm hug.

M: Do you have any advice for parents who might be having a hard time?

A: Every child is different, and no matter what kind of situation, you have to support your high-school children and encourage them according to their innate abilities.

****

This is an unusual interview: an American dad, Jerome, is interviewing his Taiwan-born wife, Esther. They have four children, one presently attending high school.

J: Please introduce yourself. What's your background both as a high-school student in your country and as a parent now in the USA? What were your parents like? Tell us about coming from another culture.

E: I'm from Taiwan. My name is Esther Wong. My parents were very liberal with regard to my education. My mom was not highly educated. Her job was to take care of us. That was it. When it came to homework and tutoring, my mom could not be helpful. My dad was a businessman, so he didn't have time to help me with schoolwork.

J: What was high school like? How about homework?

E: I went to an all-girls school both in middle school and high school. We had to wear uniforms. In middle school, there was an all boys' school next door, so that was fun. Here in the United States my kids go to co-ed schools. In Taiwan, the government provides public education for all only through middle school. We have a three-year high school, but you have to pass an exam to attend.

J: You said you had to study on your own, so how did you manage?

E: I applied myself. I liked English. At that time, American folk songs were very popular in Taiwan. I was greatly influenced by that. I was mesmerized by the songs and music.

J: Did you have pressure from your parents to do well in school?

E: No, not really. They were very liberal. I realize today that I was a good kid. We didn't have video games or computers. I only would listen to music, that's it. I studied and turned in my homework on time. My parents did not worry because I did homework by myself without distraction. I'd be sure to complete whatever was assigned.

J: What if a student needed tutoring?

E: There were schools available to prepare the middle school students in their final semester to enhance their high-school entrance exam results.

J: Did you feel if you didn't do well in school that you would be disappointing your parents?

E: I don't know. I just thought that was my job. I was a well-behaved child and student.

J: Did your parents ever get upset with you for not doing homework?

E: Never. They were open-minded to start with, and I never gave them occasion to get angry with me.

J: Were they interested in your report card?

E: When my report card came out, I always gave it to my parents. They were happy. My dad had great expectations for me.

J: Wasn't that pressure?

E: Not at all.

J: What was high school like?

E: You are assigned to varying high schools according to your test score. My test was good enough to get into the best high school.

J: What's the name of that high school?

E: Taipei First Girls High School.

J: You've lived in the USA now for seventeen years. Do you notice in the schools that the kids are given a lot of leeway? Sometimes kids will challenge their parents. Did kids talk back in Taipei, or was it a culture that was strict?

E: You're not supposed to talk back in our culture. That's disrespectful.

J: Did some kids talk back?

E: Yes, of course. Every kid's different, here and in Taipei. But I never did that. Being the oldest in the family, I felt I had the responsibility to be a role model for my sister and brother.

J: Did your parents teach you that, or was it just in your culture?

E: In my culture and in my nature. My dad was especially liberal. He would say, "Try your best," without placing pressure on me. I was confident I could achieve something special in my life. Taipei First Girls School has a unique uniform, dark green. If you were wearing this uniform, everyone in your neighborhood knew you were going to the best high school. My dad was thrilled. On my way to school, the neighbors could see me, the only one in our neighborhood attending Taipei First Girls. My dad was like, "Wow, my girl is the outstanding one in our neighborhood."

J: You did well in high school?

E: I did all right, not the best.

J: Were your parents still at peace with you regarding your schoolwork?

E: I received B's, not A's, but my parents were fine. They always felt I knew what I was doing. They trusted me and let me work things out for myself. I deserved the trust, because I was a good kid, helping around the house. I remember our uniform. The skirt had pleats. I would worry about wrinkles and iron the pleats myself. I took care of myself as much as possible and minded my own business. I did my job, so my parents didn't need to worry about me.

J: How would you describe the difference in cultures with regard to education? How do you compare your household in your high-school days in Taipei with our household today? How do you feel about how the children are doing at school?

E: Regarding my kids, of course, every parent has expectations for their children. As mixed children, Jewish and Chinese, with a father who's a doctor, most people think my children are very intelligent. Certainly, I expect them to do well. In the Chinese community, there is always pressure to show off where your children attend university. If your kids go to a good college, you feel so happy. You might feel shame if your children don't make the grade. "What happened?" Perhaps the parents didn't guide them well.

J: You feel guilty if you don't do your best to make sure the kids study?

E: Yes. I never have been a parent who wants my kids to get straight A's. I know that not everybody can be at the top. I want them to reach at least the medium level. If you cannot get an A, then B is the minimum acceptable grade. If they can achieve A's, that's great, and somehow I will give them a reward. If they improve, I'm especially happy. My attitude is from 8th to 9th grade, I ask my child to do the best he can, but starting from 9th to 10th grade, I want him to focus more on study until finishing high school. These few years can decide your destiny, the direction of your life. Of course, that's not one hundred percent true, but I always tell my kids to pay attention to study. They do not have to worry about anything else. That's their work. Their father works so hard to support them. I say, "Look at your father. He gets up early. Even sometimes, he doesn't feel like going to work, but he has to." This is his responsibility. "Same for you," I tell my kids. I say, "Study and try your best. If you think you need some help, let us know. We will get you help. But you have to put your own effort into study."

J: Would you say there is a difference between us as parents in relation to our ideas about school in the United States and your parents as you were growing up in Taipei?

E: Sure. My parents wanted to make sure I felt comfortable, but they weren't directly involved helping with homework. My mom always wanted me to have nutritious food and proper clothing. She did what she could to make me comfortable, but left the responsibility of study to me. Here in the USA, kids have so many distractions from study: TV, video games, computers. Technology rules the times. In my household, my husband and I have a different way of teaching kids. I lean toward traditional ways, but at the same time, I'm still liberal. My husband, according to his mood, is mostly liberal. In one way he's right: you don't use violence against the kids. Scolding can be all right, but not in excess.

Bamboo Bending

J: What do you mean when you say you're traditional?

E: Traditional means that if the children misbehave the parents will punish them. Some parents in Taiwan use a stick, but my parents did not. Some of the teachers in the school were mean and might physically punish you.

J: You know here in California that's illegal.

E: Of course. I remember one time in a math class in high school, some of my classmates were talking and the teacher got so angry he threw the chalk and called the misbehaving students, "pigs." I was shocked. That was so rude and insulting.

J: The difference between you as a parent and your parents, who did not put pressure on you to study, is that you do put pressure on your children to study?

E: I think parents should help make sure their kids are capable of working on their own. We have to guide our children until they can study mostly by themselves. We have to be patient with late-bloomers. Each student is different and we adapt accordingly.

J: Is there anything you learned as you were studying in Taipei that you apply to helping our children learn in the US schools?

E: In Taiwan, we spent more time in school than in the USA. Here there are many more extra activities, such as clubs in high school. Children have a variety of learning opportunities here; the system is better in the sense of being more balanced.

J: Since the children were small, you've sent them to after-school programs. Is it because you feel they should be in the school setting longer, as in Taiwan?

E: Yes and no. I wanted to keep our children bilingual (Mandarin and English), so one of the purposes of after-school programs was to support this goal. Our children spoke more Mandarin than English when they were little, and I remember our second son having some catching up to do in English, so I thought the after-school would help his reading. It did help. Many parents put the kids in after-school programs, not just because they want the extra school time, but the parents have to work, and they prefer the students have supervision and a chance to learn rather than being alone at home. So the after-school tutoring not only would help with homework, but also provided babysitting.

J: Do you scold the kids to study?

E: Sometimes my husband and kids say that, but I'm not the only one to yell at my kids to study. Other parents are also forceful. I know my children ask me why I repeat myself about study. They don't want to hear it again. I say to my children that if I told you once and you did your work, you know I will keep my mouth closed. The problem is they have this habit of procrastinating, so I have to be strong to try to get my children into action to reverse this habit. My husband wants to come home to a peaceful environment, so if I raise my voice with my kids, he will interrupt right away. When my husband and I end up arguing, my kids often feel their dad is completely on their side. When my kids don't feel the need to listen to me, I totally give up. I told my husband he is now responsible for our children's education. He may be happy to do this, but when he's tired or in a bad mood, he will tell our children to come to me. (*Laughing*) That's the story of our house; so I'm still involved even after giving up.

J: How about the issue of finishing homework before bedtime?

E: I want them to go to bed around 9:00-9:30.

J: It never happens.

E: Well at least in elementary school I had the kids in bed around 9:00 even if they couldn't sleep right away. They were not allowed to get out of bed whether they were sleepy or not. Eventually they would fall asleep. When it comes to middle school and high school, they have sports activities, so they do their homework later. Usually the latest is around 11:00 p.m., which I guess is all right. If they go to bed at 11 and get up at 7:30, they have had enough sleep. Our kids now have tennis activities, once or twice a week so I think that's healthy. The kids need exercise and some outlet for all the emotions of growing up. As a family, I'd like us to get out into nature more.

J: How do you use your leisure time and have fun?

E: I relax several ways. I love gardening. It's healthy, outdoors. I will mop the floor, clean the house. That's my way to forget about things I don't want to think about. I'll play mahjong with friends, but not too often. I watch some Chinese sitcoms from my iPad.

J: How do you make the children feel appreciated when they do well in their studies?

E: I'll give them a hug; sometimes I'll give them money, which is what the kids want nowadays. (*Laughing*)

J: How about the times you are insisting that they study harder?

E: I both praise and blame. I just tell them to study hard, that it's a competitive, global world.

J: Do you consider your son, as he gets older, to be more of a friend?

E: Yes, of course.

J: As he gets older, do you feel he is more mature with you, less rebellious?

E: Yes. I guess his dad taught him how to deal with me. (*Laughing*)

J: What do you think about volunteering? Is it important for him to be well-rounded?

E: Yes, for sure. He's involved with volunteering.

J: What do you think of Tiger Mom?

E: You mean from the book. You know she uses the traditional way to parent. She didn't completely stop her girls from a social life. She had the same idea as most parents: she'd guide her children to success. She designed a demanding schedule for them. She asked them to have certain times for study and artistic and musical practice, sleep, and meals. When the kids are younger, you have to set up a path, a schedule for them that works. When they are older, of course, they have their own thoughts, their own thinking. They can change a little, but basically they won't go too far off the track. I think Tiger Mom's way is good, as long as the parent praises the children when they do well. You can be strict, but no beating. I agree with my husband that beating is not the right thing to do. I know some traditional Chinese fathers might beat their children because they had the same treatment when they were little.

J: How important is travel for the children's education? Museums?

E: We travel a lot. It opens up their eyes, and we do our best to have them travel. We go to museums and try to keep abreast of what's available.

****

Natalie was born in China, her son in the United States, though he lived mostly in China until he was fifteen years old. A student during the Cultural Revolution and Mao's infamous suppression of education, she's a firm believer in integrating effective educational practices from both cultures, East and West.

M: What was high school like for you in China?

N: In the days of Mao, we did not value school as we do today. Maybe two or three times a week in high school, students would go out to the farms to work. I went to school in Guangdong. The school was not at all strict; education was not taken seriously because of political reasons. Yet even in this climate, the students were extremely respectful of the teachers, at least in the school setting.

M: What did your parents tell you about study at that time?

N: They had to survive; they only told me to follow what I was told to do.

M: Did you enjoy study?

N: Not early on because teachers were not allowed to make the most of the students' capacity to learn and grow intellectually and socially. It was a difficult time to be in high school. Later I came to love learning as a treasure.

M: What's the difference between high school in the USA and in China?

N: Nowadays, the kids in China usually study longer hours. My son went to school at 7:00 a.m. and came home at 9:00 p.m. It's much stricter.

M: Do you think USA high schools should have longer days?

N: Yes, I do. It's their job and students should be serious.

M: Perhaps students could start later and end the school day later? Jobs are 9 to 5.

N: In China, students also have to do homework after 9:00 p.m. If students started school later, that might help with sleep. What's important is that students actually study and do homework responsibly.

M: What could China learn from USA schools and vice-versa?

N: The USA might learn about discipline and China more about freedom to make decisions, not just to follow, but to ask questions and take part in dialogue. In China, the students are asked to follow the rules, but today's students in the USA and China, need both dedicated study and the understanding of how to use their freedom wisely in this liberal, global society. Take the best from both worlds. In my opinion, the eagerness to learn is stronger in China. Of course, nothing is so black and white, but as a general rule, American students have to learn to avoid the temptation of so many choices and stay concentrated on the goal of graduating from high school and, if possible, attend a great university. The Chinese student and parent have to be willing to complement traditional educational methods with technology and the modern insights of educational psychology and neuroscience.

M: Thanks, well said. How do you help your son with homework?

N: Academically, I cannot help him. I provide a good environment; I push him, though I try to be patient and understanding when he needs breaks. I ask that he do all his homework and really understand it. Usually he needs at least two or three hours to finish. He must study well for exams and get all A's. Then he'll be admitted to a high level university. His dad wants him to attend Cal Berkeley. There's no TV in my house because the computer is distraction enough.

M: What have you noticed about your son as he's going through the stage of adolescence?

N: I cannot bother my son too much now or he will tell me to leave his room. When he was younger, he would never say that. Now the kids are more selfish. If he needs me, he talks to me; if not, it's "Get out of my room." (*Laughing*) Sometimes I say, "This is my house, and you can get out of my house." I'm still the boss, but my son doesn't pay attention to me as he did when he was younger. I know he wants some independence; he has to earn it by working hard.

M: Are you more friends with your son as he grows older?

N: I've always treated my son as a friend, even when younger, and now in a more mature way. I'm still the parent and have authority, but I want to know what my son wants and needs in his life as he's growing. He knows I want him to have a great future. Also he'll make mistakes or not know what to do, and he's confident that, both as a mom and friend, I'll help him. We can talk to each other without being afraid of being misunderstood. It doesn't mean we don't argue, but in the end, we are on each other's side. I know some parents say not to be friends with your children; perhaps they're afraid it would keep them from disciplining their children when needed. I am happy to be friends with my son as sometimes he talks to me about private and personal matters. I know he values my opinion not just as a parent but also as a friend who listens to his side of the story, to his feelings and ideas. If I'm not his friend, he may hide important information from me. It's stressful to be a parent, but worse if you don't have the confidence of your children. They'll trust you if they feel you love and appreciate them.

M: You take care of your downtown retail business as well? How do you relax?

N: To travel is the best. But at least get out of the house, eat out, go to the shopping mall, spend time together as a family.

M: Do you encourage your son to take part in extracurriculars?

N: Music or sports would be good, but there is no time for my son to do that because of his academic after-school programs. If my son were to take art, he wouldn't have time to do his homework. I fear his GPA would suffer if he were to engage in extracurriculars. His focus is study; if he has extra time, then he can pick some activity to his liking. My son's often up until midnight or 1:00 a.m. He's taking the most difficult courses; his obligation is to learn them well.

****

Teachers need to inspire a love of learning.
—Mitt Romney's concession speech, 2012

Ginger, a doctor in China, brought her nine-year old daughter to the United States to start a new life. She has an animated presence, youthful and intelligent.

M: Where did you go to high school, and what was it like? Did your parents have a strong role in encouraging you to study or were you self-motivated?

G: I am from Shanxi Province, in the city of Taiyuan, the capital of Shanxi, close to Beijing. I went to the top high school in my city, so I had no choice but to study my best. I studied three to four hours each evening. I would go to bed at 11:00 p.m., which at that time I considered very late. I would go home from school, have dinner and study until bedtime. It was not necessary for my parents to nag me to study.

M: Now you are a parent to a sixteen-year-old sophomore in high school. What's your role as a parent?

G: In China, the student has a difficult challenge, starting from elementary school. High school seemed like college level to me. The textbooks were deep, so I needed to spend a lot of time at home to grasp meaning.

M: Are you a strict mom?

G: In China I was. I try to let my daughter in the USA find her study interesting in her own way. I do not want to push her too hard. I don't like aggression, especially for teenagers who are not open to being forced. My daughter does not appreciate parental pressure to study, so I let her find her own style. She can do her study by herself.

M: You never yell at your daughter to study?

G: No, she screams at me to leave her alone, and I do. I know she needs some distance from me.

M: Are there notable cultural differences between high school in the USA and in China?

G: Yes, there are. I learned something new from America; in China, I wanted to always push my daughter to be the top student. But when I came to the USA, I met teachers, such as her art teacher, who told me not to put too much pressure on her, but to allow her to become interested in study. My parents did not watch me and put pressure on me, but they did yell at my younger sisters to study. In China, you have to use high school to prepare for college; this is necessary for a good job in the future. So my parents were concerned that their children be good students even if it meant nagging.

M: How can we combine the best from the Chinese culture with the best from the USA in education? How can they learn from each other?

G: In American culture, the encouragement of the student is stressed. The teacher says, "You're doing great." In China, the teacher would not say, "You're an excellent student." Even if you have 99%, you'll be asked to achieve 100%. In China the student is seldom complimented. So I think the combination of encouragement and also promoting the effort to keep improving would be the best from both worlds.

M: How has your daughter become so motivated to excel in school?

G: She is more self-motivated. When I am busy working, she manages her study by herself. I am proud that she can do many things independently; that's part of becoming more mature. When we were in China, most of the children played piano. I engaged a teacher for my daughter, but she just didn't like it. I was insistent that she practice, but after six months, her dad said: "If she doesn't like piano, just forget it. It's not essential." I would make her cry with my pushing, but finally I gave up and agreed with my husband that learning to play piano is not for every child.

M: How does your daughter manage homework? Are you involved?

G: She manages. In China, I felt she could not organize her study so I did check on her. Soon after, she started being more responsible. I was very busy, but at the end of the day, I always queried about her homework. When she didn't finish, I'd feel bad. By the time we were living in the USA, the teachers always reported that she was a good student and was growing in self-confidence.

M: What's your daughter's study environment like in the home? Does she have all she needs, including quiet and study tools?

G: I want her to go to the library because it's close to her school. The library is quiet and everyone there is studying. At home, she is tempted by the world of cyberspace. This is high school and it's basically a life of study. (*Laughing*) At home the Internet is such a great attraction; I love it too. But I know when I have to work, and I want my daughter to know when it's time to study. Sometimes my daughter studies for a while, then wastes time on the Internet. She prefers to study at home, so I have to accept that she might stay up late to finish her homework.

M: I like the students to use the Internet in their study, to google for understanding their high school assignments. Some of the students in the SAT English class use the Internet on their iPads or iPhones very effectively as a tool to check information during a lesson. On their breaks, they can use the Internet as entertainment.

G: We don't always use the Internet for what we're supposed to be doing. I like to go home and watch the news on the Internet. It's fascinating. I know I should be reviewing online professional journals. (*Laughing*) That's the reason I want her to study in the library. It's less distracting and if I fall into temptation, I know she will too.

M: What skills do you want your daughter to learn besides the basic content of each subject?

G: I think my daughter is shy to speak up. She needs the chance to present herself in class, not to be afraid of being laughed at or ridiculed, but to speak. She's funny and has a good personality. Is there a course called Development of Teen Social and Communication Skills? She needs the fortitude not to give up. She says she raises her hand in class but isn't always called on to answer. She then is reluctant to raise her hand again. I hope she can learn not to get emotionally down when she's not acknowledged. I e-mailed the teacher that my daughter is trying her best to participate. My daughter received a very low grade in Participation last quarter.

M: But your daughter is assertive at home?

G: Yes. She often tells me what I should do as if she were the parent. (*Laughing*) I know she's going through a lot physically and emotionally. On the issue of sleep, I've really given up. I let my daughter sleep when she wants, but it's still hard for me. I want her to be healthy. I go to bed at midnight; she is always still up. I don't like it but I'm not trying to change her.

M: It's necessary that your daughter take a daily nap.

G: Yes, she has to. This is the cycle she's created. It's imperative to have a snack and a nap after school in order to maintain her schedule. Some teachers actually go overboard with homework; others are not strict enough.

Occasionally before I sleep, I suggest my daughter go to sleep early. She'll always say, "Not finished yet."

M: What advice do you have for parents and children who get into yelling matches?

G: My daughter does yell at me, and at first, it was a shock, because I was not used to it in China. My friend said even in China the teen might yell at the parent: "Don't bother me. Leave me alone." At the beginning, I just wanted to fight back. I was angry, and I wanted to control my own daughter. But finally I realized to fight against what I cannot really control only made matters worse. I became quiet; that doesn't mean I didn't feel hurt. But I also understand my daughter is changing and finding her own way without me. We unfortunately vent some anger on the ones we love. If she needs my support with anything, including school, I'm available for her.

M: Do you reconnect with your daughter after she's yelled at you?

G: Yes. Once the morning after my daughter had screamed at me, she sent a text, "Sorry, Mom." So that settled my feelings. She's realizing she has a bad temper. That's part of growing up, learning how to control our tempers when we don't get what we want. My daughter tells me she just cannot control her emotions sometimes. I understand.

M: What do you enjoy most about having a teenage daughter and what's the most difficult?

G: I love the times when I feel we are best friends. She talked to me about wanting to have a boyfriend; I was happy she still wanted to talk about such an important part of life. She asked how I would react if she had a boyfriend. I told her I'd be happy for her. She related that some of her friends were grounded because they had a boyfriend. I don't believe grounding for this reason is the right way. I think I'm lucky, because I know some teens won't talk with their parents. As my daughter grows up, I have to allow her to be more independent. She doesn't want to spend much time with me; she wants to be with her friends. That's the hard part of seeing her grow up. It's difficult to know when I have to let go. Before I could hug and kiss her, but now she pulls away.

M: What's your opinion of Tiger Mom?

G: I heard about Tiger Mom in China, and most Chinese parents like her very much. I've learned that Tiger Mom cannot be stereotyped, that even Tiger Mom knew when it was not good to push her child. Tiger Mother can be overly strict and demanding with children to achieve unrealistic academic or artistic goals. I believe in some cases, Tiger Moms have a goal for their child, such as to be a lawyer or a doctor, which they themselves failed to achieve. They want the child to fulfill their dreams. It depends on the personality of the kid how the strategy of the Tiger Mom works. If the child is independent, he or she will rebel. In my own case, I am not a Tiger Mom in the sense of pushing my child. Of course I encourage her, but really I'm in the background. I am a Tiger Mom in the sense that I want to provide the best learning environment for my daughter. I provide an optimal emotional and spiritual atmosphere.

M: Would you give an example?

G: Once my daughter and I had a terrible argument. I felt very bad and so did my daughter. My daughter is close to the pastor at our church, and had a healing conversation with him. She later talked to me in a calm and respectful way. We need to make peace with the very strong emotions that can overwhelm our lives. We need a friend's perspective and some help with what we cannot control by ourselves.

M: How do you handle stress?

G: I know if I'm in distress, my child will not have a peaceful home; we will argue, and that's not a healthy way to manage the ups of downs of being a human being. I need to release stress by going to the gym to exercise on the treadmill; I have two best friends with whom I can talk about my life and secrets. After talking, I feel much better. My friends can help me keep everything in the right proportion. Alone, my heart is turbulent. Sometimes I also go to a Christian church and have a conversation with our Chinese bilingual pastor about personal matters.

M: Thanks so much.

G: Really enjoyed the conversation.

7

Nourish

One jarring thing that many Chinese people
do is openly compare their children. I never
thought this was so bad when I was growing
up, because I always came off well in the
comparison. . . . I know now that parental
favoritism is bad and poisonous.
—Amy Chua

If you don't follow the rules,
then I must beat you.
—Wolf Dad, Xiao Baiyou

Xiao Baiyou (Wolf Dad) has his followers, but by no means do they include all Chinese. I reject his practice of beating a child to instill discipline. Spanking, if practiced at all, does not require a beating. Spanking at home is illegal in such countries as: Austria, Bulgaria, Costa Rica, Croatia, Cypress, Denmark, Germany, Greece, Hungary, Iceland, Israel, Kenya, Latvia, Luxembourg, Moldova, Netherlands, New Zealand, Portugal, Romania, Spain, Sweden, Tunisia, Ukraine, Uruguay, and Venezuela. Child abuse (including beating) is not tolerated, but "reasonable" forms of discipline are legal in: Canada, China, Japan, Korea, the Middle East, the United Kingdom, the United States, Taiwan, and Russia. Wolf Dad's son, Xiao Yao, respectfully but firmly criticizes Dad for his beatings. Wolf Dad, however, attributes his children's academic success to his ten years of beating them. "From 3 to 12, kids are mainly animals. Their humanity and social nature still aren't complete. So you have to use Pavlovian methods to educate them." Xiao Yao, 22, sadly doubts he had a childhood, and while he loves his dad, he also hates him. Dad devised

1,000 rules, many inane, so he had multiple opportunities to bully and physically abuse his children. Elizabeth Gershoff (University of Texas at Austin) comments on the results of her extensive studies on corporal punishment. "The more kids are spanked, the more problematic their behavior is." No human being at any age is only an animal.

Recently I received a new tutoring job, a first: teaching English to my four-year old godson, Dwight, and his mom Muoi. I couldn't imagine ever physically hurting him, even when he's being a little boy and not paying attention to his godfather's lessons. I can see using physical force only as a means to protect him from getting hurt. He's by no means a Pavlovian dog that needs the shock of physical pain to command his attention. I want him to find satisfaction and curiosity as he takes his first steps of formal learning. Naturally, he'll jump around or play sometimes. I try to create a balance between study and play; it's different each class. Neuroscientists reinforce with observable data what wise parents and educators know: teach emotional and cognitive skills, both left and right-brained, praise and encourage, use the best technology, take breaks, relax, be aware of over-parenting and over-teaching. Dwight's young brain is a sponge soaking up his experiences cognitively and emotionally. Violence encodes the brain to associate pain with learning, the opposite of what education is about. In a child's mind, violence also becomes an acceptable manifestation of anger. Throughout the stages of human growth, we record not only thoughts and explanations but sensations, imagery, and feelings.

****

Should teachers impose physical discipline on their students? I'm firmly opposed to this practice, which is now rare in the United States, but does occur. "Fifteen-year-old Taylor Santos let a classmate copy her homework and she learned the hard way never to do it again. Santos, a student at Springtown High School in Texas (one of nineteen states which allows it), was punished by a vice principal (a man) with a swift swat to her bottom using a wooden paddle. The spanking left blisters and forced her to sleep on her side that night" (*Time*, October 15, 2012). Sometimes a parent or teacher needs to be assertive but is never justified in being abusive. A few times I've had to restrain a student who was acting out inappropriately; but excessive, punitive violence is out of the question.

Viewing Wolf Dad's Internet picture with four of his children, three attending Peking University, I wondered if the smiling family harbored buried hurt. Though beating children is physical and emotional abuse in most people's eyes, Wolf Dad says beating children is not violent. However, children constantly exposed to such abusive behavior are fearful and hurt, even if it's hidden. Eventually, hopefully in a positive way, the child will overcome the ill emotional effects of the physical pain inflicted. Violence against one's person has deep psychological effects, magnified many times over if the recipient of the violence is a child. Invasive, abusive, punitive beatings and unnecessary spankings encode a sense of resentment and outrage within the person. "Spanking children can cause long-term developmental damage and may even lower a child's IQ," according to a new Canadian analysis that seeks to shift the ethical debate over corporal punishment into the medical sphere. A *Canadian Medical Association Journal* study examined twenty years of published research on the issue. The authors assert that "the medical findings have been largely overlooked and overshadowed by concerns that parents should have the right to determine how their children are disciplined" (February 7, 2012 Toronto, Reuters).

****

Watching Professor Yang teach Sophia "Juliet as a Young Girl" was one of the most amazing and humbling experiences I've ever had. . . . I no longer had to yell at Sophia or fight with her about practicing. She was stimulated and intrigued; it was as if a new world were opening up for her, and for me too, as a junior partner.
—Amy Chua

She (Lulu) played it more confidently and faster, and still the rhythm held. A moment later, she was beaming. "Mom, look—it's easy!" After that, she wanted to play the piece over and over and wouldn't leave the piano. That night, she came to sleep in my bed, and we snuggled and hugged, cracking each other up.
—Amy Chua

Yale Law Professor Amy Chua is proud of her daughters, Sophia and Louisa (Lulu). Amid multi-layered human experiences, Amy recounts successes, failures, and the will to evolve and live life fully. Some critics claim she was overly strict, and not sensitive to the need for children to play, but concede that together Amy and her American husband, Jed, are admirable, smart and compassionate parents with remarkable children. Amy tells the story of her younger sister's fight with cancer, and writes movingly about the death of Jed's mother, Florence. Birth, life and death: our lives are fleeting. With our children in mind, we somehow endow meaning to it all. Amy makes a reasonable case for being strict as well as fair and loving, taking into account modern scientific knowledge, openness to change and realistic love. A friend, Gary Schouborg PhD, was talking to me about "the positive, though risky, role of demand," which was evocative of E. E. Cummings: "My father's anger was as right as rain." Cummings is saying the relationship with his father was such that the father sometimes knew what was in the best interest of the son, who was in turn wise enough to recognize that his father's anger was warranted. A dad told me: "I never spanked my children, until one day my five-year old darted out into the street. I thought if ever a child should be spanked, this is the time. Not because I was angry, but because I needed to impress on him the magnitude of the mistake he made so he knew never to do it again."

****

Bamboo Bending

On September 17, 2012, the Pakistani government shut down access to YouTube. The purported reason was to block the anti-Muslim film trailer that was inciting protests around the world. One little-noticed consequence of this decision was that 215 people in Pakistan suddenly lost their seats in a massive, open online physics course. The free college-level class, created by a Silicon Valley start-up called Udacity, included hundreds of short YouTube videos embedded on its website. Some 23,000 students worldwide have enrolled, including Khadijah Niazi, a pigtailed 11-year-old in Lahore. She was on question six of the final exam when she encountered a curt message saying, "This site is unavailable."
—Amanda Ripley

Most young students need a push to work hard and persevere through some inevitably boring high school study. Teachers are using the Internet and new technology to make study more interesting, but students still need to focus and persist in doing the attentive work to grasp the material. Parents and teachers are committed to connect an individual student's ways of learning to academic or technical training. A small number of students leave high school to take online courses—through Cisco, Microsoft and other corporate-sponsored schools, which can lead to well-paying and satisfying jobs. Some high school students supplement classes by joining the rich online global classroom.

Dr. Eric Topol, Director of the Scripps Translational Science Institute, appeared on television to explain the importance of "wireless medicine," and the need to update personal health care, especially through the use of the smartphone. Using a smartphone-sized screen, he showed the audience the inner working of his interviewer's heart. Earlier he had attached a sensor to the man's chest. The audience watched a live video of the interviewer's four-chambered heart throughout the remaining segment of the interview. Topol said we can take a cardiogram from a modified iPhone, in the comfort of home. There are phone apps for tests using blood, urine, sweat, and saliva. An ultra-sound (Vscan) exam can be self-administered. From their offices, doctors can watch at the same time echocardiograms are being administered to a patient who is likewise viewing a screen in his or her home. Dr. Topol criticizes the "cattle herd," "wasteful," "test everyone," "mass prescribe" mentality in modern medicine. Likewise, educators are aware of analogous tendencies in our schools. Topol wants people to be part of making decisions, according to their individual needs. He credited the digital revolution with his ability to immediately check if he's over-eating carbohydrates and triggering excessive glucose. After "guilty eating pleasures," he can monitor his glucose level via a sensor on his abdomen, wirelessly sending signals that produce a reading on a screen. Today a patient can check blood pressure through wearable wireless biosensors.

Dr. Topol spoke of a new project, which will be perfected with time. A patient with heart disease can be warned ahead of time when a heart attack is imminent. The size of a grain of sand, a nanosensor is introduced into the blood stream to detect menacing cells forming on the artery lining. With information sent directly to a computer, appropriate action can be taken. Topol summarizes: "A new era of digital health care will make medicine more precise and participatory, but we certainly are not there yet." Coupled with a holistic understanding of the physical-emotional-intellectual evolution of the brain, we need likewise to employ growing technological expertise in education. Parents and teachers attempt to bring out the natural potential in our unique children. As we continue to provide a safe, healthy, and stimulating environment, both in cyberspace and in the classroom, our remarkable children-students, will acquire relevant 21st Century educational-occupational skills and habits of good character. Co-creators of a new world, our children are cherished treasures.

****

Amy Chua's *Battle Hymn of the Tiger Mother* is "a coming of age book." I was impressed that she softened her demanding "Chinese" approach after her thirteen-year-old daughter rebelled. Describing some nasty fights, she speaks of retreating (almost) as a Tiger Mother from her thirteen-year old. ("I knew I would lose my daughter, so I pulled back.") "I think it's about helping your children be the best they can be—which is usually better than they think!" Chua shares stories of being Tiger Mom, the rewarding and the harrowing, the successes and the mistakes. It's a personal story of growth, as well as an important and ongoing conversation about education and parenting. Amy has a good sense of humor ("Some writing is tongue-in-cheek"), which might be missed if the reader has overly stereotyped the Tiger as only serious. Tigers can be very playful. The quality of the family relationship matters most. I give my students more leeway when needed and more forceful and motivating prompts when required. Sometimes I can light a fire under a recalcitrant student with a well-timed talk. "Your family is providing the money and support so you can practice SAT quizzes and tests in a professional SAT class. You aspire to be accepted by an outstanding college—and there are many—so by taking the SAT workshop, you add objective proof of your commitment to gain access to the finest universities. You also can acquire and reinforce meta-skills, such as speaking and reading in front of others, basic writing, critical reading, and collaborating to achieve goals. Each class can help you organize future study, work, and socialization. You cannot succeed if you don't practice, just as you need to prepare for a mile race by running the distance repeatedly. The actual SAT test is the day of the mile race, but you need to have developed stamina and strategy by running practice tests. Be confident and focused. Visualize yourself taking the test: arrive early, be alert, ready to give your best; control your breathing; feel it as a game rather than a burden; be well rested. If prepared, you won't be seeing strange material. Have fun with it; make it a challenge to do your best. You've already been thinking through problems, memorizing and applying vocabulary in context, reading critically, understanding grammar, and writing. You've read and discussed the helpful strategies given in the SAT preparation books. Don't just practice for one or two laps and sit out the last two. I know you're tired sometimes; take breaks when necessary, but work harder; soon you'll be in a mile race. Don't spoil yourself by insisting every activity be gratifying. Commit yourself to practice what you need to know."

I don't often go on such a rant, but some reluctant students seem to bring out a sense of urgency in me. I find each student to be unique and interesting, even those who don't listen or try much. Teens are remarkable in many ways, but they need to hear the call to keep learning. I don't give up or take it too personally when the students ignore my pleas to stay on task, even when they are sometimes disrespectful. My reward occurs when students tell me of their pride upon reaching their goal of a personal SAT best.

****

Bamboo Bending

Tigers are capable of great love, but they become too intense about it. They are also territorial and possessive. Solitude is often the price Tigers pay for their position of authority.
—Amy Chua

An American dad married to a Chinese woman was telling me how his high school son sometimes argued quite heatedly with Mom about study. Dad was saying, "There are times when Tiger Mother has to let up. Look, our children are just great, full of life and their own interests, bright. We can appreciate them just the way they are. Why push them if it's harmful to their well-being?" In the old country, "The Tiger, the living symbol of strength and power, generally inspired fear and respect." Chua's Westernized children resisted the devoted obedience given by Chua to her parents. At the same time, Tiger Mom rightfully sticks to her guns about the positive benefits from the Chinese culture when adapted intelligently in the United States. We can't be controlled by our fear—which we all have as parents—that our children's immature judgment and poor choices limit their future. This is their time to learn through inevitable mistakes, and to develop during this stage of human growth. At times we have to separate our own anxieties from what's going on, perhaps saying, "Forcing my kid to change is not working; I'll change."

****

Nourish

Like an eagle, I push my child to the limit
so he can learn to fly.
—He Lie Sheng

Just as eating against one's will is injurious to
health, so study without a liking for it spoils
the memory, and it retains nothing it takes in.
—Leonardo Da Vinci

With more than a million hits, in February of 2012, Eagle Dad, He Lie Sheng, soared the Internet. He filmed his four-year-old son, Duo Duo, clad only in his underwear and shoes, running in the snow and doing push-ups. Dad explained that this was an exercise in his son's training program to develop a "masculine temperament." Were his demands excessive and emotionally damaging? Isn't there a healthy midpoint between pampering and excessive parental direction? Recently, Duo Duo, who failed to climb Mt. Fiji with his dad, was quoted: "Daddy, I want to play."

I make demands of my students for attention, organization, and practice in a healthy, supportive environment. On some occasions, the class is uniformly eager to learn, asking questions and improving study habits. In contrast, at other times I need to direct the students back to the task. Parents and teachers must adapt, seeing our children not only as the perfect embodiment of our dreams and expectations, but as unique human beings, perhaps not always corresponding to what we have in mind. Before us is a beautiful child who may not achieve all A's but has the ability to be successful, healthy and happy in life. We encourage the student to do his or her best.

A Chinese parent told me she had softened her demands on her daughter. "I ended my habit to criticize her. At first, I wanted to motivate her to try harder to please my expectations. I relaxed and found a child happily going to school in America, much different than what I experienced in China. In China, I directed her study. Now she's more in charge." Demands can definitely be too much, unreasonable and uncompassionate. I witnessed a student break down into convulsive weeping because she felt bad about not meeting the academic goals set by her parents. She felt guilty, not smart enough, but no matter how hard she tried, even with tutors, she could not achieve straight A's. "I study so hard; I have only two A's. I'm everything my parents and family don't want." Demands that don't match the teen's ability become torture for both the teen and the parent. The student may internalize a feeling of "I'm no good," but this negative self-evaluation is based on a very limited understanding of measuring what's good. Such evaluation is likely an inaccurate appreciation of the teen's capabilities and is not in the best interests of the student. Dr. Schouborg comments: "Sometimes my demand of you can call upon the best in you. It's more than an invitation; it's a version of exorcism, a calling out of dysfunctional behavior. You might say it's a demand that you be your best at the precise moment when you are ready to act but need a forceful challenge to direct your attention properly. Where demands fail is when either the demander or the demandee or both mistake where the best interests of the demandee lie at the precise moment."

****

Nourish

*I'm well aware of the fact that I'm old. By the
way, I used to say "old," but now when I'm
asked in interviews, "How old are you?" I
reply, "Well, I grew up in China in a time
when age was venerated,
so I am eighty-six years venerable."*
—Huston Smith

*I feel caught in our cultural myth that aging is
a failure, that if only I did it right I could
avoid old age, even avoid death.
What a peculiar notion!*
—Lee Lipp

A high-school senior listed "lifelong learning" as a
vital skill for the twenty-first century. "My grandpa
takes a mental fitness course at the adult school, and
he's really into it," he remarked. He is the grandson of
an octogenarian I taught at adult school in a senior
center in El Monte. My students were in their
seventies, eighties, and nineties. Some showed off
letters from the President of the United States after
blowing out a candle on their 100th birthday cake.
From 1991 to 2008, through Baldwin Park and El
Monte-Rosemead adult schools, I taught Mental
Fitness at senior centers and convalescent hospitals. As
with my present high-school students, I needed to be
flexible. I realized each senior student was one of a
kind and deserved my respect and attention. Students
varied in their cognitive ability to respond; several
were severely limited by dementias, most commonly
Alzheimer's. Some were in the hospice program.
Because of cuts in the California state budget in 2008,
the El Monte-Rosemead Adult School no longer offers
courses for seniors in convalescent hospitals; thirteen
Mental Fitness teachers and I were laid off.

Youthfully naïve in the late '60s, I blamed social
unrest principally on the older generation. I refused to

appreciate the wisdom and richness of earlier generations. Earlier in my life at age ten with nothing to do on a hot summer day, I was walking past a run-down, two-story home where Mrs. McCarthy was pruning bushes in her front yard. She lived alone, and had the reputation of being an unapproachable shrew. Not afraid to wield a shotgun, she instilled fear in the kids who pranked her. On this particular occasion, she asked me to help her lift bush trimmings into a wheelbarrow, which I did while casting a suspicious eye on her, remembering some kids called her a *bona fide* "witch." Apart from her unsmiling wizened face, I found nothing sinister about her. Mrs. McCarthy's musings on plants, flowers, trees, squirrels, rabbits, muskrats, dogs and cats captivated me. She never spoke about other people except saying that a group of "wretched boys" had thrown rocks at her dogs. After I finished the job, she invited me to enjoy freshly baked cookies and cold milk. That began our friendship. I started visiting her, walking up the long driveway, knocking on her door and gaining entrance into mesmerizing conversations and enchanted rooms. I looked at her photo albums and inspected her "favorite contraptions." Opening a painted music box inlaid with white-spotted black and orange butterflies, I was greeted by a melody that brought delight to Mrs. McCarthy's noticeably softened face.

Elastic even as we age, our brains can "stretch" and "coordinate" just as we flex and harmonize our bodies. Neuroscientists call this ability of the brain to keep itself fit, "brain plasticity." Dr. Daniel Siegel writes about doing exercises to strategically target a particular portion of the brain. "The answer is attention ... moment-to-moment neural activity can gradually become an established trait through the power of neuroplasticity." Teachers coach students to focus attention on a present task, to keep their minds alert. Some convalescent homes and senior adult programs provide computer exercises. Seniors do exercises to listen more attentively, focus and concentrate, improve the ability to process and remember progressively larger amounts of information. They distinguish varying sounds, and remember details from stories, improving the speed with which they process information. Seniors review history or geography or watch clips from old movies, and they are asked to remember setting, characters, and actions. Hospitals and senior centers use the Internet to explore cyberspace, research information of interest, e-mail and chat.

****

The magic of neurobics lies in the brain's remarkable ability to convert kinds of mental activity into self-help. . . . Experience the unexpected and enlist the aid of all your senses in the course of the day. . . . Involve one or more of your senses in a novel context; engage your attention; break a routine activity in an unexpected, nontrivial way. . . . If you are right-handed, controlling a pen is normally the responsibility of the cortex on the left side of your brain. When you change to writing left-handed, the large network of connections, circuits, and brain areas involved in writing with your left hand, which are normally rarely used, are now activated on the right side of your brain. Suddenly your brain is confronted with a new task that's engaging, challenging, and potentially frustrating.
—Lawrence Katz and Manning Rubin

Neurobiologist Lawrence Katz, co-author of *Keep Your Brain Alive, 83 Neurobic Exercises*, describes neurobics as "creating new and different patterns of neuron activity," exercises "to keep the brain agile and healthy." Some of the high-school students find computer brain exercises—some similar to "Mental Fitness" exercises for seniors—useful in learning to focus. They use computer programs such as "Lumosity" to sharpen cognitive functions of attention and perception; doing neurobic programs can be useful and fun for students. The field of brain-training, with such companies as CogniFit, SharpBrains and Posit Science, is growing. These programs have to be tried out, practiced and well-crafted enough so they continue to capture the student's attention. Brain exercises may not necessarily increase one's IQ, but they serve to tune-up the brain. Although not a magic pill as some advertise in exploitive, exaggerated ways, brain exercises can improve cognitive skills. In 2005, Swedish neuroscientist, Torkel Klinberg used brain imagery to present evidence that brain training can alter the number of the brain's dopamine receptors. Dopamine is instrumental in learning and other cognitive abilities. Directing full attention to study along with the ability to relax and rest are two indispensable skills.

It's unrealistic to expect all courses in high school to be interesting. The students need some exposure to various courses to know what they really want. It is in the best interest of the student and society in general that the student be exposed to basic academic disciplines. That way society and the student know where the students' future contribution lies. Is demanding study against the will of the student who is "without a liking for it" harmful? Many have gotten through dull material in order to reach a goal. You might have to "pretend" to be into what you're studying, and just do it. Unexpectedly, maybe you'll find yourself engrossed and challenged. In the future, by all means go for what excites you.

Nourish

****

We created an atmosphere where older adult students could, according to their capacity, stay physically and mentally active. We offered exercise, Tai Chi, music, dance, singing, arts-crafts, bingo, history, geography, language arts, mathematics, puzzles, trivia, video documentaries, and educational movies. We had conversations about health and nutrition in these Mental Fitness classes. Doctors and dieticians recommended seniors adjust their diets to include food and vitamins that increase blood flow and nourish the brain, lower inflammation, and improve alertness. Research proposes that practicing activities such as educational "trivia," learning a language or playing a musical instrument helps build reserve brain cells to fight against failing mental ability.

Sadly, several students already suffered from advanced Alzheimer's and other dementias that greatly limit memory and cognition and may manifest in behavioral abnormalities. Teachers in collaboration with nurses, doctors, administration and staff continued to interact and reassure the suffering student, ravaged by Alzheimer's terribly sad progressive diminishment of mental capacity. Such students were often confused, disoriented, incoherent, alienated, angry, withdrawn, deteriorating. Their words did not seem to express their thoughts. Some were "just out of it." One of my students greeted me each morning saying with a perplexed look: "I can't remember what I forgot to remember to tell you." Her daughter would visit her in class, but had to remind her each time that she was her daughter. She enjoyed going to class, especially singing and humming old songs and playing catch with a soft fabric ball. However, there were times when she would sit with a blank expression on her face. J. Madeleine Nash, *Time* magazine chief science correspondent, writes: "Imagine your brain as a house filled with lights. Now imagine someone turning off the lights one by one. That's what Alzheimer's disease does. It turns off the lights so that the flow of ideas, emotions and memories from one room to the next slows and eventually ceases" (*Time* magazine, July 17, 2000). Though we could not stop this deterioration in our students, we did our best to accompany and care for them.

There are some false alarms regarding Alzheimer's. An estimated 350,000 Americans suffer normal pressure hydrocephalus (NPH), a curable disease that mimics Alzheimer's memory loss, unsteady gait, and lack of bladder control. NPH manifests when the brain loses its ability to reabsorb the clear fluid that surrounds it. NPH is treated by reducing brain pressure; a dime-sized hole is drilled into the skull to implant a shunt to drain the fluids. For 85 to 95 percent of NHP sufferers, this surgery successfully restores memory.

At whatever level, for as long as possible, the teachers interacted with the seniors. Domesticated animals were brought into a convalescent hospital-hospice. Some of the students didn't want to be (and would never be forced to be) close to any animal, yet many did and found it great fun and excitement, like having an instant, loving "buddy," in what can be an alienating, colorless environment. A ninety-three year old student happily played with a chubby cuddly kitty. For some years at Baldwin Park Adult School in a facility for the deaf, I worked with friend, Belva Watkins. Belva would bring friendly cats and an occasional dog to visit our classroom. The students enjoyed petting, feeding and holding them. The animals had a calming effect.

Our family was lucky to share our life with a loving Golden Labrador Retriever, Maya. Greeting her family members with wails of excitement, she couldn't contain her happiness to be with us as if we were returning from a long journey. Rolling on her back, through her eyes she'd ask us to rub her belly. My wife called Maya the family psychologist. I agree with Samuel Butler: "The great pleasure of a dog is that you may make a fool of yourself with him and not only will he not scold you, but he will make a fool of himself too." Leave it to Japan to manufacture endearing, affectionate robot animals called Paro that interact with those suffering dementias. With big warm eyes and sweet faces, they are: dogs with wagging tails, electronic seals mimicking sounds of Canadian seals, soft purring cats, and furry black-and-white panda bears.

8

Grow

Take the attitude of a student, never be too big to ask questions, and never know too much to learn something new.
—Georgia O'Keefe

I want to serve. I want to serve the people. I want every girl, every child, to be educated.
—15-year-old Malala Yousafzai,
February 4, 2013

Our survival as a global community requires the evolution of a relevant education for all children. Worldwide, people champion Malala Yousafzai, a precocious 16-year-old Pakistani girl who wished to attend school contrary to a tyrannical Taliban dictate. She's electrifying the call for women's rights. On October 9, 2012 an assassin boarded her bus and shot her in the head just behind her left eye. The religiously-fanatic Taliban intended to kill her in retaliation for her support of female education. Two other children, now the world's children, were wounded. Many voices are being heard, including loud protests in Pakistan: "Stop practicing discrimination against women"; "Using your religion to justify such hate has to be called out by the world community"; "Senseless violence is not true practice of Islam." The Taliban still wish to execute her. How crazy and cowardly is that?

During what Wolf Dad misguidedly calls the Pavlovian stage of development, at age eleven in 2009 Malala Yousafzai began blogging for the BBC Urdu Service to expose Taliban atrocities against women. Through the Internet, forces are mobilizing and support is growing for her just cause. "People think

'Western values' is wearing jeans and sipping pop. Malala was doing none of that. All she said was: 'Would you be kind enough to reopen my school?' This is what the Taliban thinks is a 'Western value.' This is not a Western value. This is a universal value" (Educator Murtaza Haider, Ryerson University, Toronto). From her hospital bed, Malala told her dad she wanted to become a politician. I think she'll be whatever she wants; she's a shining star of youth, a symbol of resistance against those who deny education to girls and women. Malala is strong; at the same time, she's a vulnerable teen receiving the embrace of the global community. Saying she would persist in her cause, Malala left the hospital on February 8, 2013. As Chelsea Clinton reported, "Malala is now where she wants to be, back in school. The Taliban almost made Malala a martyr; they succeeded in making her a symbol. The memoir she is writing to raise awareness about the 61 million children around the world who are not in school indicates she accepts that unasked for responsibility as a synonym for courage and a champion for girls everywhere" (*Time*, April 29/May 6, 2013). Written with Christina Lamb, Malala's book *I am Malala* was #4 on the *New York Times* Best Seller's List on October 27, 2013. Educators, parents, and students in the United States should not take our freedom to go to school for granted.

Malala recognizes that her celebrity has brought added suffering to her former classmates as they endure Taliban retribution over Malala's emergence as one of the leaders in the global human rights movement for universal education. The violence and threats of the Taliban, coupled with the lack of educational opportunities, and the presence of American drones all contribute to make life unbearable for those left behind.

****

The right to an education is sacred. On September 4, 1957, as a thirteen-year-old I read about Orval Faubus, the segregationist governor of Arkansas, and the courageous fifteen-year-old Elizabeth Eckford. Along with law enforcement officers, Faubus blocked Elizabeth from crossing a line to attend Central High School in Little Rock. A terrified Elizabeth was separated from other black students who would also be turned away in their efforts to desegregate Central High. They were Carlotta Walls, Jefferson Thomas, Ernest Green, Gloria Ray, Melba Pattillo, Terrance Roberts, Minnijean Brown, and Thelma Mothershed. There was defiant refusal to welcome these black students. A kind white woman, Grace Lorch, escorted Elizabeth to a bus and safety. This Little Rock integration crisis was given a lot of press. Our teachers, the sisters of St. Mary's in Norwalk, Connecticut, invited us to write letters in support of these courageous, young blacks.

On September 25, President Eisenhower ordered twelve-hundred soldiers from the 327th Airborne Battle Group of the 101st Army Airborne Division to escort the nine African-American students into the school. Some Central High students offered active support, but there was always some racial taunting. Minnijean Brown was dismissed from school when she dumped her bowl of chili on the head of a heckling, taunting student. The black cafeteria workers clapped. In 1958, Ernest Green would be the first black student, in a class of six-hundred-and-two, to graduate from Central High. No one clapped for him as he walked across the stage with his diploma. On September 10, 2007, *compadre* Dave Van Etten sent me an article from the *San Jose Mercury News* about the ongoing friendship between Melba Pattillo and Dave's former Santa Clara University boxing teammate, Marty Sammon. Marty was one of the paratroopers sent by President Eisenhower to protect the nine black high-school students. Melba was fifteen years old, Marty twenty-three. Melba appreciates the soldiers who protected her for six weeks. She recalled: "The troops are here. We are going to live; we're going to make it. . . . I celebrate this man every day of my life." Marty, who volunteers as a boxing referee and had a part in Clint Eastwood's film *Million Dollar Baby*, says, "I'm filled with enormous respect for those kids. None of them quit."

****

Once we realize that people have very different kinds of minds, different kinds of strengths—some people are good in thinking spatially, some in thinking language, others are very logical, other people need to be hands on and explore actively and try things out—then education, which treats everybody the same way, is actually the most unfair education. Because it picks out one kind of mind, which I call the law professor mind—somebody who's very linguistic and logical—and says, if you think like that, great; if you don't think like that, there's no room on the train for you.
—Howard Gardner,
Harvard Graduate School of Education

A student said it was impossible to comprehend physics. What could be done to make physics more accessible? How could he envision its key concepts and experiments? He found You-tube presentations of physics helped him grasp the subject. "I can see it, so I understand it." Jet Propulsion Laboratory's visual strategist, Dan Goods "once drilled a hole through a grain of sand to demonstrate the size of our galaxy, and then put that grain of sand in six rooms of sand that represented the universe" (Patt Morrison, *Los Angeles Times*). Teachers are aware that students learn through the combination of verbal-linguistic, logical-mathematical, musical-rhythmical-auditory, visual-spatial, and bodily-kinesthetic strategies. My student said he was unable "to grin and bear it" through a thick textbook he did not comprehend. Through videos, he created a mental landscape into which his textbook gradually fit. Finding his personalized "way to be smart," he began highlighting texts, inserting blank pages to write and illustrate with multicolored pens. He would add pictures and drawings, making his book a "TV set." Some of my students learn best by collaborating and co-tutoring, solving problems by talking them out with a group; others are more intrapersonal, and self-taught. Some students talk and walk (kinesthetic) when doing lessons. Linda Wong, author of the textbook, *Essential Study Skills*, writes: "Muscles also hold memory, so involving movement in the learning process creates muscle memory." We have varying intellectual strengths that affect how we represent reality in our minds. Many students master high-school history by including the visual media arts to understand the ideas, times, characters and events through the passage of time.

At the start of a high-school semester, a student bemoaned the loss of two innovative teachers laid off due to state budget cuts. In protest, she was excusing herself from studying hard.

"It sounds like your dissent keeps you from giving the teachers you now have a chance."

"It's not fair that two of my newer, more respected, prepared and enthusiastic teachers—after two years of teaching—were handed their pink slips. Others who are less competent are now my teachers. Why should I study so hard? Some teachers don't even correct papers but give a preconceived grade."

"You think the two outstanding teachers are the only avenues for you to learn? The system has its defects for sure. In a business, poor performers would be fired, but it's more complex in a large unionized school system. And teachers are different, having their own abilities to teach and communicate; students often have varying views of the same teacher. Once, while talking to an old high-school classmate, I told him I didn't particularly like a certain teacher. He responded that he was his favorite teacher, because the teacher took him aside and taught him how to organize his study, a skill he took with him into a successful career in business. Take the whole of your resources into account and follow your instincts to make the best use of them. Complement your classes with online courses. You have other teachers you connect with. Aren't you the principal teacher?"

"I'm mad at the school to let this happen. You don't seem to sympathize. What about empathetic skills? I do understand that I'm also my own teacher."

"I sympathize; I just don't agree with your sense of proportion. You are wasting too much of the energy you need to pursue your education by being angry at what you can't change."

"That's how I feel. It's still not right. I'm passionate about having creative teachers, whether they're young or old. Why doesn't the business of education value the most dynamic teachers? Any other worthy enterprise would not allow the best new talent to get away."

"OK, you got me. Anyway, no excuses for not studying hard and making sure you enjoy it at the same time. Why not? You have access not only to your own able teachers, but to teachers from around the world."

(*Laughing*) "I knew you were going to say that."

****

Grow

*Integral education combines character and
personal development ... academic
performance and qualities of kindness,
creativity, etc. aren't mutually exclusive.*
—Willow Dea

*Life is like riding a bicycle.
To keep your balance you must keep moving.*
—Albert Einstein

Global awareness is an essential skill as outlined in the core competencies of the *21ˢᵗ Century Skills Framework*, a coalition of government education offices, businesses, and professional organizations. Think globally, implement locally; develop intellectual and empathetic skills. "Use critical thinking and problem solving to understand and address global issues; learn from and work collaboratively with individuals representing diverse cultures, religions and lifestyles in a spirit of mutual respect and open dialogue in personal work and community contexts; understand other nations and cultures, including the use of non-English languages." Living through the Civil War, American philosopher, Charles Sanders Peirce (1839–1914) saw young men risk their lives without hesitation to help others in horrendous situations; he concluded that empathy is part of our human nature, that it's built in us, however buried it may be. In *The Global Achievement Gap*, Tony Wagner (Innovation Education Fellow at Harvard's Technology and Entrepreneurship Center) urges educators to develop young people's capacities to innovate such as growing a willingness to work collaboratively.

****

Bamboo Bending

The only thing that you absolutely have to know, is the location of the library.
—Albert Einstein

I encourage students to read magazines and books and to use the library, even though they may not become avid readers. Some tell me reading opens new worlds for them; they catch the bug of reading. They speak about expanding their points of view through vicarious experiences. Others tell me they are allergic to books.

****

All forms of motivation do not have the same impact on creativity. In fact, it shows that there are two types of motivation—extrinsic and intrinsic, the latter being far more essential for creativity. . . . Extrinsic motivation, comes from outside a person— whether the motivation is a carrot or a stick. . . . But passion and interest—a person's internal desire to do something—are what intrinsic motivation is all about.
—Teresa Amabile
Entrepreneurial Management Unit,
Harvard University

At times, I gratefully witness students overcome distractions and study with inquiring curiosity. My students are learning skills they'll need long after they've left the raft of an SAT score on the shore of yesterday. Parents and teachers can reinforce "the intrinsic motivation of play, passion, and purpose versus the extrinsic carrots and sticks." We help children discover what they want, motivating and supporting them so they work diligently to develop and prepare themselves through study. Students are experimenting, looking for what works for them. They aspire to be creative as well as to learn technical, procedural, and intellectual knowledge. Amabile summarizes: "To produce real innovations, knowledge in and of itself is necessary but not sufficient. You also need 'creative-thinking skills'—the innovator's skills that allow you to ask the right questions, make connections, observe, empathize, collaborate, and experiment. Finally, you need *motivation*." When I coached basketball in high school, I found that the players' love for the game energized them as a team. Their excitement was my inroad to getting their best efforts in practice. I'd teach them to run patterns but also to be free to calculate instinctively when it was advantageous to be creative, to adapt. Today's students likewise need stimulation, generating excitement about learning relevant skills, as well as the flexibility and imagination in applying such skills to constantly changing conditions.

An indignant student once complained vociferously about his history teacher. I asked what they were studying. "The Civil War," he answered. We started to talk.

"Isn't that interesting to you?" He said it was a fascinating topic but the teacher killed it. Without looking up, the teacher just read from the book, putting everyone to sleep.

"Who provides the most important spark to get your brain into action?"

"I know it's me, but the teacher has some responsibility to get our attention, right?"

"OK, I agree, but when he or she doesn't teach well, can't you read along, view the illustrations, take notes, and think about the topic as the text is being read? I also don't like to hear someone who doesn't read with feeling, who doesn't present material dynamically; but sometimes, as you've noted, we need to provide our own extra effort and energy to learn well."

"Or I can just learn it later and get some rest in class."

"That may be wasting a chance, don't you think? You have to decide if this strategy is the best for you. You do need rest. Does resting certain times in class really help you study more effectively outside of class? Both high-school students and college students now take Internet classes, so you won't necessarily have to go to the classroom, though the majority of your classes will remain on campus. But for now, why not do your best to delve into the Civil War despite the teacher's shortcomings?"

****

The story of Finland is the story of survival.
It is eloquently captured by Aleksis Kavi's
first Finnish novel, Seven Brothers,
which was first published in 1870.
It is a story of orphan brothers who realized
that becoming literate is the key to happiness
in life. Since those days, reading has been an
integral part of Finnish culture.
—Pasi Sahlberg
Ministry of Education, Helsinki, Finland

Pasi Sahlberg's *Finnish Lesson* praises Finland's regard for its teachers who usually count on an accommodating and interesting environment in which to teach. Finland's teachers have the power and flexibility to control the curriculum and student assessment in a high-tech and well-read community. Unlike in most of the United States, vocational teachers work in upper-secondary schools. Educational reform is coming globally, infused with some educational wisdom from Finland. It's time to jump on board.

To complement classwork, serious students sometimes ask for tailored homework exercises at a pace that matches their needs and capacities. They want to learn the SAT English material, practice tests and go over the results; at the same time, they improve intellectual and social-emotional skills, learning to pay attention, think, process and apply knowledge faster and better, imagine, and be creative. They realize learning is not confined to the classroom, even though face-to-face interaction with the teacher and classmates is very valuable. Some students are not eager to participate in class, much less ask for extra SAT exercises to take home. "My brain is so slow. I can't take it. It's so boring."

As do other SAT teachers and coaches, I sometimes give general suggestions about rest, diet, stress, breathing, and focus. Breathing with a sense of one's own presence is simple, but like SAT tests, must be practiced. Take a few deep breaths when feeling distracted, just as a basketball player does before shooting a free throw. At the beginning of an SAT test, one student told me she quietly breathed deeply three or four times, filling up with air with the in-breath by expanding her belly and filling her lungs, then contracting the belly on the exhale like pushing air out of a balloon. When she felt unfocused and nervous before a test, she'd practice this method. Students usually benefit when they prepare themselves physically and motivationally by straightening their postures and challenging themselves to do their best in the game of the SAT. Alert and confident, they attack the ten sections of the SAT test as carefully as possible, one problem at a time.

⁂ ⁑ ⁑ ⁕ ⁜ ⁜ ⁕

Bamboo Bending

*Imagination is more important than
knowledge. For knowledge is limited, whereas
imagination embraces the entire world,
stimulating progress, giving birth to evolution.*
—Albert Einstein

A parent asked: "What are contemporary educators saying to students and parents about collaborating to make high-school education more relevant?"

To students: Make the effort to strengthen yourself in this magnificent stage of human growth. With study and practice, whether academic or vocational, you will find a unique interest, which will give your life meaning and a direction toward a career. You have a responsibility to give school an honest effort, just as we parents and teachers have the obligation to make learning accessible and relevant. Stay on course. Keep the sense of fun in life. You have four years to master the high-school curriculum to the best of your ability. Your brain—with its capacity to think and understand— is extraordinary. Your body is in peak condition. You can learn to think logically and become poised and confident emotionally. When you study, bring back your attention as distractions arise; practice directing your mind, and develop your will and intention. Establishing better self-control by setting boundaries for yourself, you learn to discriminate longer-term satisfactions from immediate rewards. You become both socially sensitive and grounded as your own person, living and integrating experiences, finding how to manage relationships and your emotions. Navigating the world of high school, a student realized: "I'm seeing it's only me who can live my life, which is not always a safe feeling, but exciting and fun at the same time. I'm into what I'm doing." In the United States for only two years, a student worked assiduously to get a decent SAT score. Her practice scores were low for a year and a half but she finally made a large enough jump in her score to be accepted at a university. She said she never thought she could do it, but "somehow I never gave up. I learned the power of my will to achieve what's important to me. It feels good to achieve the goal."

To parents: You are supporting your children physically by keeping them safe and healthy, and psychologically by loving them as they develop in unique ways. While assuring they have an excellent education, take care of yourselves as well. Sometimes we do too much and never slow down. Parents teach more by the way they live than by what they tell their children to do. I've seen parents so worried, irritable and stressed about their children that they forgot about their own needs for leisure, recreation, and time with family and friends. Though living at home, the teenager wants some independence and decision-making; teens need their own space and so do parents. We parents have to relax our urge to overly control our children. We have to accept that our children have needs for quiet breaks and times to socialize and play. With mental and emotional refreshment, we can all create a resourceful inner life, which translates into a happy daily life.

The January-February 2011 cover of *Utne Reader* featured Marge Simpson, dressed in a blue uniform and red bandana like Rosie the Riveter, World War II icon, a working woman flexing her right bicep. Created by Howard Hiller in 1943, the image promoted political-social issues, such as women's rights. "Getting America Back to Work. We can do it." Though our education system is bent, we can recoup lost confidence in America's ability to invigorate high-school education and beyond. As the world of possibilities rapidly expands, lifetime learning has become both a necessity and hopefully an enjoyable journey.

Bamboo Bending

*It is no tragedy to think of the most successful
people in any field as superheroes. But it is a
tragedy when a belief in the judgment of
experts or the marketplace rather than a belief
in ourselves causes us to give up . . .*
—Leonard Mlodinow,
The Drunkard's Walk

Sometimes students bring up the subject of stereotyping. "Are we Asians all inscrutable, wise, classically serene, super students and lousy drivers? I want to be myself, not a caricature. I'm even a mystery to myself: teen Chinese girl and woman, immigrant, artist, high-school student preparing herself for university. I have my own experiences and reflections, and must be true to them and to myself. Don't tell me I am this way or that, or that I love school because I'm Chinese. Perhaps I don't love school at all." Most of my students dislike and speak out against stereotyping based on race or sexual orientation. "It's not rational, and it's not compassionate." When I went to high school no one mentioned homosexuality; today we understand the reality and dignity of differences, and the human right of love whether among heterosexuals or gays. Several years ago, at Baldwin Park Adult School, a distressed teen came into our computer-lab classroom where some high-school students studied alongside adult students. Tears in his eyes, breathing heavily to calm himself down, he quietly asked if I'd talk to his friend in the parking lot. Outside, I was dismayed to see a beaten and trembling former student. He had been violently attacked because he was gay. He said he was lucky he had strong family support. These days, despite some discrimination, students are more open and accepting of the human condition. There are clubs in high school that foster understanding between heterosexual and gay teens.

Seared disgracefully in America's memory is the tragic story of hate directed against gay, twenty-one-year-old Matthew Shepard. On the night of October 6 and into October 7, 1998, Matthew was tied to a split-rail fence, robbed, pistol-whipped, and tortured. Matthew's attackers fractured his skull, leaving him to die. Eighteen hours later, he was discovered by a cyclist who first thought he was a scarecrow. He died from his torture on October 12th. Addressing anti-gay hate crimes, in 2008 the Matthew Shepard and James Byrd Jr. Hate Crimes Prevention Act was passed, a federal law against crimes directed at lesbian, gay, bisexual or transgendered people. Dennis and Judy Shepard created The Matthew Shepard Foundation to honor Matthew in a manner appropriate to his dreams, beliefs and aspirations. The foundation aspires "to replace hate with understanding, compassion and acceptance, through a variety of educational, outreach and advocacy programs."

My class once asked me which country's students impacted me the most. I reflected on being an ESL and Living Skills teacher in the late '70s and early '80s for a government humanitarian program designed principally for Vietnam War refugees. Meeting students from South and North Vietnam, Laos and Cambodia broadened my connection to different cultures. The Cambodian refugees I taught and continue to teach today are remarkable, having physically survived the tyrant Pol Pot and his Khmer Rouge soldiers (1975–1979). They lived through fear, work, hunger, loss and the unspeakable torment of genocide. Beginning a new life in America, they revealed stories of how the government demanded a passive and subservient role from them. One had to pretend to be foolishly naïve and ignorant. Tyrannical governments and individuals defile the value of the individual human being and attempt to destroy his or her thirst for freedom. Cambodians could not wear eyeglasses or use an educated and polite form of speech. One of my students was eighty-years-old, a father of six. Many from his immediate family had been slaughtered in Cambodia; he would enter the classroom and bow to me. He exuded a feeling of gentleness, yet an underlying strength, living with dignity after crushing heartbreak. I would bow to him as well.

Under the ruthless Khmer Rouge, Cambodian children who reported parents' transgressions were given more food. The government sought total control by destroying the family. The government forcibly separated children from their parents. Between October 1979 and May 1980, 164,000 Cambodian refugees arrived in Thailand. During the Khmer Rouge's reign, 1.7 million Cambodians, a fourth of the entire population, were executed or died from forced labor, disease, and starvation. Through their tragic and heart-breaking stories, Cambodian students inspired me with their enthusiasm and resilience. They told me of their dreams for their children's education, and hope to prepare them for a happy life in the United States. The love of our children and grandchildren in all cultures makes the world go round.

I became aware that different cultures, lifestyles, and ways of thinking affect the immigrant's education. I noticed that Asian cultures emphasized family in its societal organization. The way the elderly are usually treated is a prime example. Two or three generations of family commonly live together. They tend to be less outgoing than Americans. This contrasts with the American preference for one's own space and privacy, yet American parents also willingly sacrifice for their children. My parents told me similar stories of immigrants who arrived at Ellis Island with heads held high and a sense of humor still intact despite their past suffering and current apprehension. Officials would ask, "Have you been promised a job?" Most replied, "I intend to get a job as soon as possible." Those "huddled masses," some fleeing repressive governments, sought freedom. I had a similar positive impression of the Vietnamese, Laotian, Hmong, and Cambodian refugees.

****

After the fall of the Khmer Rouge in Cambodia, a monk, Maha Ghosananda, "Gandhi of Cambodia," served, counseled and consoled the survivors of "the killing fields." Ghosananda was one of three thousand monks still alive out of sixty thousand. The devastated Cambodian survivors carried tremendous hatred, suppressed resentment, and an almost unbearable sorrow. Most were hopeless and distraught. With love, the venerable monk Ghosananda taught them the words of Buddha (similar to those of Jesus and other great religious teachers): "Hatred is never appeased by hatred; by love it is appeased; this is an eternal law." How can one possibly let go of such malevolence perpetrated by the Khmer Rouge? As difficult as it is to forgive an enemy, bitter hatred causes the hater physical and psychological harm. By nature we are meant to love, not hate. Lewis B. Smedes writes: "To forgive is to set a prisoner free and discover that the prisoner was you." Ghosananda encouraged people to change themselves, get healthy, both physically and spiritually, even if they could not change others.

Not every Buddhist monk is like the compassionate, non-violent and wise Ghosananda. Seventy percent of Sri Lanka's 20.4 million are Buddhists, including bellicose groups of monks who in 2012 attacked Christian communities fifty times. "The Buddha Power Force (Bodu Bala Sena), one of the violent Buddhist groups, recently asked its followers to 'defend the country' from Muslims and Christians" (*America*, January, 2013). In Myanmar and Thailand, belligerent monks instigate violence and prejudice against Muslims. "Like adherents of any other religion, Buddhists and their holy men are not immune to politics and on occasion, the lure of sectarian chauvinism. . . . It's hard to imagine that the Buddha would have approved" (Hannah Beech, *Time*, July, 2013). Horace Mann astutely observes: "Do not think of knocking out another person's brains because he differs in opinion from you. It would be as rational to knock yourself on the head because you differ from yourself ten years ago."

****

Students have asked me to share some teaching and volunteer experiences with older adults in a hospice program. As early as 1000 BCE, there were healing sanctuaries for the dying in Greece. Developed in the 1950s in England, the modern hospice movement assists the terminally ill in living their days as comfortably as possible, free from impersonal, institutional and technological dominance. Dying is terrifying for most of us. Hospice care establishes a respectful atmosphere that eases emotional, social, physical, and spiritual stress. The most influential model of modern hospice care is St. Christopher's Hospice in Sydenham, England, founded in 1967 by Dr. Cicely Saunders, its medical director from 1967 to 1985. The wards and rooms at St. Christopher's are filled with photographs, personal items, flowers, and plants. Patients pursue familiar interests and pleasures. There's an acceptance of the naturalness of dying, with the opportunity of families, including children and pets, to be with the patient. Cicely Saunders passed away at age eighty-seven in the hospice she founded. In more than ninety countries, hospice care—with varying levels of quality—is now well established.

Grow

Zurich psychiatrist, Elisabeth Kubler-Ross, came to the United States in 1958. As eccentric as some of her ideas later became, I always considered her a guru for hospice workers and volunteers. She passed away in 2004, but left twenty books, recordings, and videos which are widely studied. When Elisabeth first worked in New York, she was appalled that dying patients were often shunned and even, at times, abused. "Nobody was honest with them." She made it a point to sit with terminal patients and listen. She wanted the patients to have the confidence to air their "inner-most concerns." The need to be listened to is shared by all human beings. Hospice workers have told me of the satisfaction of establishing mutual relationships infused with patience, understanding, and interest in the dying individual. Elisabeth is noted for delineating five stages of the dying process: denial, anger, bargaining, depression, and acceptance. Elisabeth advised that the dying need unconditional love, no matter what the person is going through. There are no blueprints for the process of dying. Whether at home or in a hospice facility, patients and their families want reasonable dominion over pain control, treatment and environment. In hospice, there's respect for privacy, a communicated appreciation of goodness and dignity, free communication, and an opening to the spiritual needs of the individual as he or she defines them. Several in hospice ask for a priest, rabbi, minister, imam, monk or other clergy to visit them.

In 2002, Ken Ireland, whom I met after sitting in a meditation group he led at the Y.M.C.A. in the Tenderloin of San Francisco, invited me to visit Maitri (Sanskrit for "compassionate friendship"), a hospice for AIDS patients in San Francisco. Along with Issan Dossey, Ken and others founded the hospice in 1987. I was impressed by the staff and patients who created a warm, "at home" environment where both caregiver and patient deeply listened to each other. The ample

231

kitchen had a signed, framed photo of Elizabeth Taylor who had visited and encouraged the residents. Golden light danced on the fresh green plants in the hallways and communal areas. I was reminded of Camus: "The great courage is still to gaze squarely at the light as it is at death." Since opening in 1987, Maitri has been the final home for more than 900 people who lived with AIDS. "We strive to provide the type of care that each of us would like to receive at the end of our lives—care that is dignified, non-judgmental, and unconditional. We hold dear the principle that each resident has the right to determine the degree of choice and awareness with which to experience life and death."

I visited a dying former student whose family had invited a few members of their church choir to sing in the hospital. She was at times barely aware of what was going on, but for some moments responded through her eyes—appreciative and soft—as the singing filled the room. She was holding her son's hand and slightly moving her lips to the melodies. For those who welcome it, music can be uplifting, calming, and uniting for all in what might often be a frantic environment in which a loved one is dying. The National Center for Music Therapy in End-of-Life Care is based at the State University of New York at New Paltz. For a patient whose breathing is arduous, skilled music therapists would start by singing fast and loud, matching the patient's labored breaths. Then, there is a gradual slowing, softening of the music that calms the patient. There's another movement called "Threshold Choirs," which was started in San Francisco by Kate Munger. Choirs are invited into hospices, hospital rooms and homes where they sing to the terminally ill, some of whom may not even be conscious. "We walk not into the night; we walk up toward the stars," they might sing. Kate confers with the patient and family to ensure the music corresponds to the patients' tastes. She tells the story of a nurse who wanted her group to sing for a male patient drifting in and out of consciousness. During the singing, the man suddenly opened his eyes and yelled: "Stop it! What the hell do you think you're doing here?" In hospice, good intentions are never enough. Kate says lullabies are requested the most.

I went to see a former teacher, ninety-three-year-old Rev. "Pops" Silva, a Jesuit priest in hospice. He told me he didn't expect to live much longer. With a curious spirit and glint in his eyes, he related that even in his eighties, he was teaching Shakespeare in an adult-school program. Pops was pensive, still savoring a diminishing life, reading Shakespeare, devoted to God and people. He recalled sweet moments of his teaching career with me. Annoyed at his declining memory, he said, "It's all going away." He had a gigantic Shakespeare Concordance plunked regally on his mechanical bed. I mused it is fortunate to share our beds with the one we love. I remember his clear, emotional, lively expression of Shakespeare: "It is not in the stars to hold our destiny but in ourselves," and "To thine own self be true, and it must follow, as the night the day, thou canst not then be false to any man." I pushed a wheelchair-bound Pops to late morning Mass. Later we hugged our final good-bye; he died shortly after.

****

People will be most creative when they feel motivated primarily by the interest, satisfaction, and challenge of the work in itself—and not by external pressures.
—Teresa Amabile

Over the years, students have asked: "How do I know what I really want?" I have quoted experts who speak of the need to slow down and experience quiet times, allowing deeper unconscious processes to work and then emerge in consciousness. Students further query, "What keeps me from my heart's desire?" Gary Schouborg, PhD mentions three barriers against getting what we want: over-extending; only achieving what others expect; and dreaming without exercising our will power. "To the extent that we do not understand the concerns of others, we are prisoners of our own limited resources; to the extent we don't know what we want, we are prisoners of our own impulses, and to the extent we cannot negotiate differences, we are prisoners of unnecessary conflict."

Students have had similar discussions in the classroom and with counselors; they are told to be aware of fantasies, dreams, fables, and desires both in themselves and in the characters they read about in literature. Students might be asked to remember a personal experience that gave them a significant sense of satisfaction and accomplishment. In a writing exercise, they relate two or three of these experiences. A student told of how exhilarating it was to be outdoors in nature; another said she was attracted to art and felt confident and proud of her paintings. Emotion—emanating from our deep unconscious processes—can inspire us to make the effort necessary to achieve our goals. Teachers and parents want the high-school student to learn responsibility, the ability to engage and "respond" constructively, intellectually, and emotionally with others and within.

We hope our children will gain practical knowledge and also experience the mystical, "the power of true art and science . . . to wonder and stand rapt in awe" (Albert Einstein). We are working with others by listening, negotiating differences, limiting conflict and clarifying our concerns, so we can attain both common and personal goals. On a December 4, 2012 PBS news show, a commentator said, "Training is for

Grow

the known; education for the unknown." Perhaps in the past we could tell our children what to expect; but in our ever-changing world, families, institutions, and communities are preparing our students to face even the unexpected. We are evolving, continually renewing ourselves to adapt to the environment and spirit of the times—values such as inclusivity, integration, multi-culturalism, high technology, psychological savvy and spiritual health.

****

Education opens our eyes, our ears . . .
it tells us where delights are lurking . . .
convinces us that there is only one freedom of
any importance whatsoever—that of the
mind—and gives us the assurance, the
confidence, to walk the path our mind—our
educated mind—offers.
—*Iris* (2001 movie)

Traditionally youth have endured rites of passages into puberty, in order to be tested morally and emotionally. The child is socially recognized as transitioning into sexual-social maturity. This is a limited time of self-reflection leading to an increasing responsibility for self-control and decision-making. Rites of passage for teenagers come during the healthiest cycle of life in terms of strength, reaction time, and an optimal immune system. Rites can have many forms: puberty; a new school, classes; mentors; birthdays, making (or not) school teams, school plays; speech and debate; trips away from home, volunteering; first dates; getting a driver's license, a first car; report cards; awards; inevitable disappointments and accomplishments within high-school culture; bar mitzvahs; confirmations; quinceañeras; graduating from high school; being accepted

235

by a college, technical and/or academic; and entering the job market.

Every Fourth of July, an Apache tribe holds a four-day rite of passage for thirteen-year-olds, which tests endurance and moral growth, ending with an all-night dance around a ceremonial fire. The adolescent has little sleep and food and is required to be stoic throughout the process. It's a time to step away from ordinary time and touch latent consciousness, waking up to a sense of individuality and responsibility, to engage the gift of life more profoundly. After the dance, the teenager is presented with a morning star feather. Belgian anthropologist, Arnold Van Gennep describes how all cultures have ways for the teenager and society to deal with passages into puberty. In my time, the car was a metaphor for both risk and a connection to social life, school, and employment. What characterizes the growth required by the adolescent? What is her or his main challenge? Teens are learning to relate and listen, but at times with uneven, seemingly exaggerated behavior. This is a natural stage of developing functions of the mind: to focus, think, empathize, control inordinate impulses, build positive habits, and mature emotionally-socially.

I saw students on the last day of high school riding their bikes, pumping their arms, and shouting. Gleeful girls were screaming and laughing in anticipation of summer break. Showing off to the girls, a teen gunned his car, rocking to loud music at the signal light. All seemed appropriate enough; there was an underlying feeling of positive fun. Good young people, relieved for some moments from high school pressure, feeling their oats. These youngsters will rule the world.

Afterword

Often an afterword details how a book came to be written or how the author focused on a particular topic. Since Morgan Zo Callahan has already illuminated these matters so wonderfully in *Bamboo Bending: An Educator's Changing Corner of the Universe*, I'd like to comment on the spirit of the man whose book you have just put down.

Morgan is that rare individual who learns from whomever and whatever is before him. With a seemingly bottomless appetite for knowledge, he focuses (often through interviewing others or interrogating himself) on Chinese culture, Latin American life, Buddhism, neuroscience, Special Education, child prodigies, beauty in nature, the Black Madonna, his mother's struggle with death, friends who have enlightened him, dysfunctional families, teenagers, and Einstein's wisdom. His mind ranges over Tiger Moms, sleep, volunteerism, missed opportunities, pranking, neurobics, Fellini's *La Strada*, Matthew Shepard, the diminishment caused by rape and racial disparagement, and Rod Serling's "The Twilight Zone." His short sections on Alzheimer's and AIDS care are illuminating.

John L. Allen, senior correspondent and Vaticanologist for the *National Catholic Reporter*, recently wrote of Pope Francis's "revolution," using an image that immediately reminded me of Morgan's beautiful spirit. Allen said, "Plates are shifting at a deeper level." In Morgan's case, tectonic plates have indeed been shifting far below the work he has undertaken with students who struggle toward authenticity and personal courage, and far below his attentive care for them. His involvement with Matraca and Acteal, the world's poor, the US education system, Buddhist mindfulness, and Christian compassion all shed light on what is going on below the surface of his persona and underpinning life itself. He is always learning, interpreting, and affirming the talents, positive growth, and enthusiasm of his students. That is how his own journey is defined.

I offer Morgan, with all the sincerity and love I can muster, the following poem that I wrote a few years back; it captures, I believe, some of his attention to detail and love of life in all its mystery and wonder.

Don Foran
http://donforan.webs.com

Particularities

The smell of newborn babies,
Salt air, the way one's eyes
Light up—these unique particularities
Are the very heart of the universal.
How then, having been educated
By things we see and feel,
Do we yet fail to reverence earth,
Loving its every copse and pool,
Its every tremble, tang, and spark?
We long for love and fail to comprehend
Manifold loveliness. Life is in our hands,
But we must explore our heart of hearts
To understand its worth.

Appendix 1

Resources for Teachers & Students

Four Frameworks:
> Integrated Workforce Skills in the High School and Adult Classroom

1. Equipped for the Future (EFF): http://eff.cls.utk.edu/default.htm
2. Partnership for 21st Century Skills (P21) http://www.p21.org
3. National Career Development Guidelines (NCDG): http://cte.ed.gov/acrn/ncdg.htm
4. Secretary's Commission on Achieving Necessary Skills (SCANS) http://wdr.doleta.gov/opr/fultext/document.cfm?docn=6140

Additional Resources

1. Arlington Education and Employment Program (Virginia) http://reepworld.org
2. Asian American Civic Association Communicating at Work http://aaca-boston.org/caw
3. California State Library http://libraryliteracy.org/staff/rg/curriculum.html
4. Florida Works National Work Readiness Credential Mini-Course http://www.floridaworks.org/minicourse06.pdf
5. I-CANS—Integrated Curriculum for Achieving Necessary Skills http://literacynet.org/icans/index.html
6. Integrating Career Awareness into the ABE & ESOL Classroom

http://sabes.org/workforce/integrating-career-awareness.pdf

7. Internet4Classrooms Career and Technical Links (career guides/lesson plans) http://www.internet4classrooms.com/career_tech.htm

8. Latino Adult Education Services "Tierra de Oportunidad" http://www.otan.dni.us/webfarm/laes/

9. Michigan Adult Education PD Project (Preparing workers for 21st Century) http://maepd.org/lib-preparingworkers.htm

10. Work-Based Learning Connections http://wblconnections.com

11. The Learning Edge http://www.thewclc.ca/edge/

12. California Career Zone http://www.cacareerzone.org/index.html

13. Career Explorer http://careerexplorer.net

14. Jobcentral http://www.jobcentral.com

15. Mindopia: Careers in Focus http://www.mindopia.com

16. Vocational Information Center http://www.khake.com

17. http://amychua.com

18. Open Education Data Base http://oedb.org (150 Resources to Improve Writing; online schools; 10,000 free online courses; financial aid; career options)

19. The George Lucas Educational Foundation
http://www.edutopia.org
(What Works in Education: Evidence-based K-12 Learning Strategies; Social and Emotional Learning; Multiple Intelligences; The Heart-Brain Connection: The Neuroscience of Social, Emotional, and Academic Learning; Creativity and the Imaginative Mind; Schools That Work)

******

10 Big Ideas for Better Classrooms:
Striving To Improve Public Education

Students:
1. Engage: Project-Based Learning
2. Connect: Integrated Studies
3. Share: Cooperative Learning
4. Expand: Comprehension Assessment

Teachers:
5. Coach: Intellectual & Emotional Guide
6. Learn: Teaching as Apprenticeship Schools
7. Adopt: Technology
8. Reorganize: Resources

Community:
9. Involve: Parents
10. Include: Community Partners

Appendix 2

Alzheimer's Disease Resources

I have a personal investment in learning as much as I can and supporting research, which will result in a cure for Alzheimer's. My biological mother died of Alzheimer's.

It's vital that we detect the early stages of Alzheimer's so we can begin treatments before it is too late. Medicines are in the market and in development that help prevent memory loss during the early stage of the disease. Two promising eye tests, the Retina Amyloid Index by Neurovision and Sapphire II by Cognoptix, detect Alzheimer's indicators as many as twenty years before the onset of symptoms. The tests monitor the presence of amyloid plaques (a protein deposit) on the retina. The retina is formed from brain tissue as the fetus develops. Neurovision's co-founder, Keith Black, Chairman of the Department of Neurosurgery at Los Angeles Cedars-Sinai Medical Center, explains: "The key for having an effective treatment for AD is early detection. You want to prevent those brain cells from being killed or dying in the first place."

The Sapphire II measures photons, light particles, when scanning the eyes. Carl Sadowsky, medical director of the Premiere Research Institute, Palm Beach Neurology, summarizes: "The amount of photons captured directly correlates with the amount of amyloid in the eye."[3]

---

[3] http://www.dailymail.co.uk/health/article-2397005/Eye-tests-detect-Alzheimers-disease-20-years-symptoms-develop.html

Alzheimer's Association

http://www.alz.org

There is a search box to find any chapter of the Alzheimer's Association in the United States. It includes a 24-hour help line: 1-800-272-3900. Free book available: *Playbook for Alzheimer's Caregivers* by Frank Broyles, University of Arkansas.

This site also includes:

Informational Resources (e.g., "What is Alzheimer's?" "How to cope with Alzheimer's should you suffer it")

Programs for Caregivers, Families & Individuals with Alzheimer's

The following drugs are commonly used, sometimes in combination, to treat Alzheimer's, delaying early to moderate Alzheimer's for 6–10 months for 50% of patients; there are newer drugs becoming available. Vitamin E is also prescribed by some doctors. Beta blockers (out-of-favor blood pressure drugs) have shown some promise to protect against the memory loss and mental functioning of the aging brain. Physicians urge people to keep their blood pressure under control because it has a cumulative effect on the brain. Another experimental treatment for early Alzheimer's is implementing a brain pacemaker.

Cholinesterase inhibitors, which prevent breakup of acetylcholine, chemical messenger for learning and memory: Aricept; Excelon; Razadyne; Cognex; *Memantine* (Namenda), which regulates glutamate, chemical-carrying messenger among brain's nerve cells involved in learning and memory. Prescribed for moderate to severe Alzheimer's.

Variety of Relevant Articles

Message Boards/Live Chats

Help for locating Senior Housing

Today there is a movement in the USA called "Aging in Place" where seniors stay in their homes and receive medical care. However, many seniors, especially with more advanced Alzheimer's, usually need to live in nursing facilities.

How to enroll in Medical Alert & Safe Return Program (to help a person with dementia who wanders away be reunited with the caregiver, via a pendant or bracelet with a 24 hour emergency response phone number & access to personal health records)

Alzeimer's & Dementia Weekly
http://www.alzheimersweekly.com/2013/07/which-type-of-dementia-does-she-have.html

American Society on Aging
http://www.asaging.org
Since 1954, this association has been committed to enhance the "knowledge and skills of those who seek to improve the quality of life of older adults and their families." A multidisciplinary group of professionals addresses the physical, emotional, social, economic, and spiritual aspects of aging. They publish three magazines: *Aging Today* (issues that professionals face today); *Generations,* a scholarly quarterly journal; *ASA Connection* which updates relevant issues. Various seminars are offered online such as: "Comprehensive Geriatric Assessment"; "Planning and Coordinating Care for People with Alzheimer's"; "The Legal and Ethical Issues of Aging"; "The Role of Physical Activity in Reducing Falls: Best Practices for at Home and in the Community."

By 2050 people in the USA afflicted with Alzheimer's is projected to reach 13.8 million, with a projected cost of $1.2 trillion dollars. Presently, if we live to eighty-years-old, half of us will suffer Alzheimer's or another dementia. "Scientists aren't sure how it starts, but they believe it causes plaques and tangles to form in the brain, slowly killing neurons and causing the entire brain to shrink.

Between 60% and 80% of dementia cases are believed to be a consequence of Alzheimer's, according to the Alzheimer's Association" (Joseph Serna, *Los Angeles Times*, February 7, 2013). Caregivers and family members become more patient once they understand that this disease isn't something the patient can control.

Fisher Center for Alzheimer's Research Foundation)
http://www.alzinfo.org
- Mission: Funds over 85 scientists in the USA with partnerships in 117 other countries
- Directed by Nobel laureate, Dr. Paul Greengard at The Rockefeller University in New York City
- Research & News
- Publishes *Preserving Your Memory* magazine, with care-giving tips and strategies for healthy living
- Explains the 7 stages of Alzheimer's: normal; normal forgetfulness with aging; mild cognitive impairment; mild Alzheimer's; moderate; moderately severe; severe.
- Resource Locater for Continuing Care
  —30 types of health care professionals available with a search by name, state, city or zip code (e.g., Elder Law Attorneys, NAELA; Geriatric Care Managers; Hospitals; Hospices; Long-term care ombudsmen; medical supplies; Medicare, Parts A & B; Physicians; Rehabilitation hospitals; Skilled nursing facilities.)

American Association of Homes & Services for the Aging
http://www.aahsa.org
"Our 5,700 member organizations, many of whom have served their communities for generations, offer

the continuum of aging services: adult day services, home health, community services, senior housing, assisted living residences, continuing care retirement communities and nursing homes."

- Aim to make available healthy, affordable and ethical aging services
- Advocacy, Policy & Government (for nursing home transparency and improvement)
- Aging: The Facts for the USA
  —By 2026, 65 year-olds and up will double to 71.5 million
  —among people turning 65 today, 69% will need some form of long-term health care
  —by 2020, 12 million older Americans will need long-term health insurance
  —16,100 certified nursing homes (private rooms average $213 per day, $77,745 year; semi-private rooms, $189 per day, $68,985 per year)
  —39,500 assisted living facilities ($2,969 per month, $32,064 per year; with added fees for Alzheimer's, other dementias, $4,270 per month, $51,240 per year) (Also cf. **Assisted Living Federation of America** http://www.alfa.org)
  —2,204 continuing care retirement communities ($2,672 per month, $32,064 per year; $60,000 to $120,000 buy in)
  —300,000 units of Section 202 affordable senior housing (average wait, 13.4 months)
  —40% of long-term care is from private funds
  —Medicare covers rehabilitation services after an individual is discharged from a hospital; pays 19% of all long-term care spending

Bamboo Bending

—Medicaid (for low-income individuals) pays 49% of all long term care spending
- Conferences; Learning opportunities; Newsroom, Online Communities, Publications & Research
- Career Opportunities; Career Resources, including websites representing career specialties in the Aging Service field

American Health Care Association
http://www.ahca.org
- A non-profit federation of affiliated state health organizations, together representing more than 10,000 non-profit and for-profit assisted living, nursing facilities, developmentally disabled and sub-acute care providers
- This federation provides care for more than 1.5 million elderly and disabled individuals nationally
- Based in Washington D.C., it advocates for changes to improve the standards of services in long-term health care

Eldercare Link
http://eldercarelink.org
- Helps the public find qualified local elder care providers and senior services, and provides a questionnaire to match needs to available services, which will then be made known by e-mail and phone calls, community resources/information sought by caregivers
- Online collaborative community for family caregivers to help them communicate, organize, support parents or other care recipients

SNAP for Seniors—Tool to Search for Senior Housing
http://www.seniorhousinglocator.org/

- Senior housing available in one's location (with an explanation of the types of senior housing)
- Assisted living & residential care; independent living & retirement communities; nursing care & rehabilitation; continuing care retirement communities (CCRC) & multi-level care facilities
- Resources: educational booklet; relocation services; glossary; government & non-profit agencies; health-related organizations; helpful links; placement/transition coordination; geriatric care management; legal assistance;
- Home care & hospice

UCLA Center on Aging
http://www.aging.ucla.edu

- Started in 1991, the center has the "mission to enhance and extend a productive and healthy life through preeminent research and education on aging."
- Focused on Southern California, but its research and information may usefully be extended to the USA
- Promotes community education and life-long learning
- Memory Training
- Senior scholars; Annual research conference; Technology & Aging conferences
- Community meetings

60780547R00162

Made in the USA
Charleston, SC
05 September 2016